BEYOND THE

Red Sauce

CLASSIC ITALIAN COOKING WITHOUT TOMATOES

SECOND EDITION

MATT FINARELLI

To Jasmine,
All the best and
Buon Appetito!

For Susan.

With all my love, affection, and risotto.

Contents:

Acknowledgments

It's always difficult for me to know where to begin listing all the people I want to thank for their invaluable help in putting a book like this together. I'd almost have to write another book in order to mention everyone individually, and to explain all they've done for me.

I guess I should begin with my grandparents and the love of Italian cooking – and the love of being Italian – that they instilled in me. It was the beginning of a life-long love of food that brought me to where I am now. And, of course, my mother deserves great thanks as well, since she's the one who taught me that cooking is not just guesswork, but rather a collection of techniques that must be perfectly executed in order to achieve great – and repeatable – results.

Thanks so much to all my culinary instructors – both in culinary school and in the restaurants where I've worked. All of them taught me something new and important about the culinary world, and helped shape me into the chef I am today. Each time, I was shown new and exciting aspects of cooking, working in restaurants, running businesses, and teaching others how to cook. Whenever I entered a new situation or job, I felt I already knew everything I needed to know for that job, yet without fail, I was shown there was so much more to learn every time. I thank you all for making me a better chef.

As for putting this book together, I have to thank my two wonderful editors, Paula Jacobson and Sheilah Kaufman. Sure, it's hard to have every one of my recipes picked over line by line, but the resulting collection here is really something fabulous, and it's because of them that these recipes read so well. And special thanks to Amy Riolo who not only introduced me to Paula and Sheilah, but who also took the time to answer my many, many questions about what it takes to write a cookbook. She helped me take a vague idea for a book, and focused it into the book you're holding in your hands right now, and I owe an incredible debt of thanks for that.

Additionally, the writing and testing of over 100 recipes is more than I can do in my own small kitchen, so I want to thank these recipe testers who took the time to cook up the draft versions of the recipes in this book in their kitchens and report back to me on how it went: Blythe Allman, Diana Bolsinger, Andrea Carroll, Linda Erlandson, Peggy Finarelli (thanks again, Mom), Bernard Henry, Betsy Ickes, Kelly Kane, Linda Komm, John Lawrence, Mel McLaughlin, Brianne Miers, Natalie Murray, Chrystal O'Hanlon, Shane Pielli, Lynne Plante, Katie Venit and Sheila Way. Thank you all for suffering through the process of cooking unfinished recipes, and having to deal with the consequences. This book is full of great recipes thanks to you and your great feedback!

I owe a great deal of thanks to Darren Santos for taking the wonderful photos of the food on the cover and of me for this book.

And of course, I'd be nowhere without my wonderful wife, Susan. I've never known anyone who has supported me so completely and thoroughly through everything I've done; yet isn't afraid to tell me when something I'm making isn't working. It's amazing to have someone in my life who's so good to me and so good for me. I could never have done any of this without her.

Introduction

Growing up with an Italian family, I was taught the pleasures of cooking and of enjoying great food. I developed a love for all the world's cuisines at a young age, but I always seemed to find myself most drawn to Italian food and cooking.

When I became a chef, my very first job was at a café whose sole purpose was to push out as much pasta in a lunch shift as possible. But the chef had an incredible eye for detail, and I learned that even in a fast-paced environment, it was possible to get things exactly right each and every time. A sense of pride in the food you make is what it takes to turn out great dishes.

As I advanced in my culinary career, I began creating my own dishes with the same sense of pride and attention to detail that I learned from the chef at that café. It wasn't until I started creating my own original Italian dishes that I felt how strongly my heart was invested in the innovative process.

After a while, I realized that I was making the same kinds of dishes over and over when I was thinking about "Italian" food. My Italian cooking had fallen into a rut; I don't think I'm the only one who has felt this way. No disrespect meant to my family, or any other Italian-American family in this country, but all too often when we talk about cooking "Italian," it's just shorthand for "smothered in tomato sauce."

That's where this book comes in. I did **not** write this book because of a hatred of, or allergy to, tomatoes – I <u>love</u> tomatoes. I'm enamored of their robust sweetness. There is no smell in this world that compares to tomatoes picked fresh from the vine. That aroma whisks me back to my childhood and conjures happy memories of hot summer evenings on the porch with a loaf of crusty Italian bread, sopping up the last juices of the freshest tomatoes imaginable mixed with balsamic vinegar. All I'm asking is please don't think I dislike tomatoes. I would hate to think that they feel that I'm somehow slighting them by writing this book.

The point of this book, and the reason I wrote it, is to expose how much incredible traditional Italian cooking is out there that doesn't involve tomatoes. Mind you, these aren't recipes that classically have tomatoes where I simply omitted them. I'm not trying to make a "tomato-less" Pasta alla Norma in this book; certain dishes require tomatoes, and to leave out the key ingredient would be wrong on every level. Rather, these recipes combine beautiful flavors and ingredients from all over the peninsula, using a wide collection of traditional and innovative ingredients – except tomatoes. Seeing as how the tomato isn't even native to Italy, it wasn't hard to find other foods that people have loved and enjoyed there for many years.

Now that my intentions are clear, I share my collection of recipes with you in this book. Use it as a great reference for all kinds of different Italian dishes, or make an entire meal using the menu suggestions. Surprise your friends by telling them ahead of time that you're making an Italian feast; and then after the meal, over a round of cappuccinos with Limoncello gelato, ask them if they noticed that anything was missing. They'll all agree that your meal was certainly Italian, and definitely delicious. But I'd be willing to bet that none of them will notice what was "missing" until you tell them!

All that aside, take the time to enjoy these dishes, and play around with them! This is not the final word in creating Italian food; it's just meant to get you thinking about all the different ways that Italians enjoy their meals. If you can't get to Italy – which you should try to do as often as possible   then the next best way to enjoy the culture is through a sampling of the cuisine. I'm hoping that this book will make the culture and flavors of Italy come alive for you in a whole new way, and spark some great innovations of your own!

Buon Appetito!

Menu Suggestions

Sometimes it's hard to know what dishes go together well when cooking from a single cookbook. I often find myself opening two or three books because I didn't know there were great pairings available to me within the covers of one book. So in order to help you out with some ideas, I humbly offer a few ideas:

Sunday Brunch

Sunday Family Dinner

Keeping Warm in Winter

The Joy of Spring

Summer's Bounty

Romantic Dinner for Two

Christmas Eve Feast

Antipasti

Simply put, this is the Italian version of appetizers. They are the dishes that come before the first course, which is typically pasta; hence the name *antipasti* ("before the pasta"). The wide variety of antipasti that are available across Italy never ceases to amaze me.

It's not that a meal needs to have something come before the first course. The typical person who has just enjoyed a full Italian meal is rarely walking away from the table hungry. But, sometimes, a little something to wake up the senses and act as a preview of things to come is a welcome treat!

You could take the recipes here in a totally different direction. An array of these dishes could make up a meal by themselves! Similar to the *tapas* tradition of Spain, a series of small antipasti served with a wide range of delicious Italian wines could make for a wonderful late lunch or early dinner. Of course, this is the section you want to be looking at when you are asked to bring something to a cocktail party.

Most of all, this is the section to skim through to get ideas of where to begin your meal. The journey of a thousand miles starts with a first step, and these recipes are the ones that can start your journey into the Italian kitchen.

CROSTINI

Making crostini is arguably one of the best uses for that leftover bit of bread you have at the end of a dinner party. Simply slice the rest of the loaf into thin slices, place them all in a plastic bag in the freezer, and you can make these quick antipasti any time you like! I toast these breads until they're very crisp, so it doesn't matter if the bread has been in the freezer for a month or two. As with any antipasti presentation, variety is the key; so try making a bunch of different types next time you're entertaining!

CROSTINI WITH A TANGLE OF BALSAMIC-ROASTED PEPPERS
The longer you let these ingredients marinate together, the more you will be rewarded for your patience! The soft peppers on top of the crispy toasted bread are a delight to behold, and a tempting contrast in texture and flavor.

Serves 4-6

1 red bell pepper

1 yellow bell pepper

1 orange bell pepper

3½ Tablespoons extra virgin olive oil – plus more for brushing

2½ Tablespoons balsamic vinegar

3 sprigs fresh thyme

1 sprig fresh rosemary

½ teaspoon kosher salt

¼ teaspoon freshly ground black pepper

1 narrow loaf Italian or French bread (something crusty), cut into ¼- inch thick slices – about 24 in all

Whole fresh basil leaves (as small as possible) – for garnish

- Roast peppers according to directions on page 179. When cooled, cut the peppers into ½-inch wide strips.
- In a bowl, combine olive oil, vinegar, thyme, rosemary, salt, and pepper. Add pepper strips and toss to combine.
- Cover the bowl with plastic wrap and let marinate in the fridge for at least two hours, overnight if possible.
- Preheat oven to 400° F.
- Place bread on a baking sheet and brush lightly with olive oil. Bake, turning once, until lightly browned on both sides, about 8 to 10 minutes.
- Take the bowl out of the fridge, and discard herb sprigs.
- To assemble, use a fork to twist a collection of peppers together, and then top the crostini with the twisted peppers. Garnish with basil leaves and serve.

CROSTINI WITH PESTO AND RICOTTA

This is our first foray into the world of pesto; and, of course, it won't be the last. Wake up the senses and palates of your guests with pesto before the pasta course! Since these crostini are assembled after baking, if you are taking them to a party, you should probably pack the bread, topping, and garnishes separately and assemble the crostini there.

Serves 4-6

¼ cup fresh whole milk ricotta

½ cup Fresh Pesto (page 55)

Kosher salt

Freshly ground black pepper

1 narrow loaf Italian or French bread (something crusty) – cut into ¼- inch thick slices, about 24 in all

3 Tablespoons olive oil – plus more for brushing

2 Tablespoons pine nuts – toasted

24 small fresh mint leaves

- If ricotta is especially wet, spread the ricotta on a double layer of paper towels. Lay another 2 paper towels on top, and press down to remove excess moisture from the cheese.
- Preheat oven to 400° F.
- Combine ricotta and Fresh Pesto in a bowl; add salt and pepper to taste.
- Place bread on a baking sheet and brush lightly with olive oil. Bake, turning once, until lightly browned on both sides, about 8 to 10 minutes. Place toasted bread on a large serving platter and spoon a generous teaspoon of ricotta mixture on each slice.
- Garnish crostini with pine nuts and mint leaves. Serve immediately.

CROSTINI WITH GORGONZOLA

These crostini must be baked with the topping on, so it is harder to take these with you to a party – better served at your own home when you're the one doing the entertaining. Since the topping is baked on, you'll want to slice the bread a little bit thicker than for other crostini recipes so they'll be sturdier.

Serves 4-6

2 Tablespoons pine nuts

5 ounces soft mild Gorgonzola – at room temperature

2 Tablespoons minced fresh basil

Freshly ground black pepper

1 narrow loaf Italian or French bread (something crusty) – cut into ½-inch thick slices, about 16 in all

2 teaspoons honey – for garnish

- Preheat oven to 375° F.

- In a skillet over medium heat, or in a toaster, toast pine nuts until lightly browned. Transfer nuts to a cutting board and chop them into a fine powder.

- Combine nuts, Gorgonzola, basil, and pepper to taste into a paste in a small bowl. (You can make this ahead and refrigerate this mixture for up to 2 hours.)

- Place bread slices on a baking sheet, spread about 1 Tablespoon cheese mixture on each slice, and bake until the bread edges are browned, about 8 to 10 minutes.

- Remove from oven, garnish each *crostino* with a dot of honey, or more to taste, and serve warm.

CROSTINI BIANCHI

These "white" crostini offer a nice contrast to other crostini on an appetizer plate. The topping must be made at least 2 hours ahead to let the flavors blend, but wait until right before serving to put the topping on the crostini so the bread does not become soggy. Feel free to garnish them as you like, just be sure that you garnish them with something, so you don't just have a white topping on top of white bread. Remember, looking good – both for the chef and the food – is a major part of Italian cooking!

Serves 4-6

½ pound fresh whole milk ricotta

8 anchovy fillets

1 clove garlic – chopped

1 teaspoon fresh lemon juice

2 Tablespoons extra virgin olive oil – plus more for brushing

Freshly ground black pepper

1 loaf Italian or French bread (something crusty) – cut into ¼ inch thick slices, about 24 in all

12 black olives – sliced (optional, but if you use them, be sure to use high-quality olives such as Kalamatas, and pit and slice them yourself)

Fresh flat leaf parsley leaves (optional)

- If ricotta is especially wet, spread the ricotta on a double layer of paper towels. Lay another 2 paper towels on top, and press down to remove excess moisture from the cheese.
- Puree ricotta, anchovies, garlic, lemon juice, and olive oil in a food processor until creamy. Transfer to a bowl.
- Let mixture sit in fridge, covered, for at least two hours (up to 8).
- Season mixture to taste with pepper.
- Preheat oven to 400° F.
- Place bread on a baking sheet and brush lightly with olive oil. Bake, turning once, until lightly browned on both sides, about 8 to 10 minutes.
- Spread ricotta mixture on bread slices, top with olives and/or one parsley leaf if desired, and serve while bread is warm.

CROSTINI WITH GARLIC-SAUTÉED RAPINI

This recipe is a great way to use rapini, one of the fabulous side vegetables I talk about later in this book. If you have leftover rapini from the night before, it reheats beautifully into this antipasto/snack for the next day. Of course, this dish is so good on its own, you'll want to make it every day just to enjoy the way these flavors go together!

Serves 4-6

½ pound rapini (broccoli rabe) – rinsed and dried

1½ Tablespoons olive oil

2 cloves garlic – minced

Kosher salt

Crushed red pepper

1 loaf Italian or French bread (something crusty) – cut into ¼-inch thick slices, about 24 in all

Extra virgin olive oil

Zest and juice of 1 lemon

Freshly grated *Parmigiano Reggiano* – for garnish

- Prepare rapini by removing leaves from stems. Keep leaves whole. Chop off florets, keeping them whole. Chop stems into ½-inch pieces.
- In a large pot of boiling salted water, cook stems for about 2 minutes, and then add leaves. Cook for another 5 minutes, then add florets. Cook for an additional 3 minutes and drain in a colander. Lightly press out any excess water.
- While rapini is cooking, heat olive oil in a large skillet over medium heat.
- Add rapini and garlic, and cook, stirring frequently, for about 20 minutes, allowing the flavors to come together.
- Season to taste with salt and red pepper.
- While rapini is cooking, preheat oven to 400° F.
- Place bread on a baking sheet and brush lightly with olive oil. Bake, turning once, until lightly browned on both sides, about 8 to 10 minutes.
- When rapini is done, and still warm, divide it among the crostini. Garnish with olive oil, salt and red pepper to taste, and a light dash of lemon zest and juice.
- Top with Parmesan and serve warm.

Bruschetta

Arguably the most famous of Italian antipasti, these open-faced sandwiches are served on thicker slices of bread than crostini, and the bread is typically brushed with olive oil, grilled, then rubbed with garlic. I personally think the rubbing with garlic is not the best (or easiest) way to put garlic flavor into a bruschetta, so I usually omit that step and instead incorporate the garlic into the topping. What follows is a collection of recipes that all work perfectly on thick slices of grilled bread. I grill only one side of the bread and place all the toppings on that grilled side. Make any one, or prepare a varied collection for your next large party!

Bruschetta with Roasted Red Peppers and Fresh Mozzarella

This bruschetta is simple yet full-flavored. Be sure to use real buffalo milk mozzarella if you can, and use the best olive oil you can get your hands on. Roasting your own red peppers is always best, although jarred ones can work here in a pinch.

Serves 4-6

2 balls fresh buffalo milk mozzarella

1 roasted red pepper (page 179)

8 thick slices good quality Italian bread

2 Tablespoons extra virgin olive oil – plus more for garnish

10-15 fresh basil leaves – torn if large, left whole if small

Kosher salt

Freshly ground black pepper

- Preheat a grill or your oven's broiler.
- Cut mozzarella balls into thick slices; set aside.
- Slice red pepper into ½-inch strips.
- Brush bread slices with olive oil, and grill or broil on just one side until nicely browned.
- Top with mozzarella slices and red pepper strips. Garnish with olive oil and basil leaves. Season to taste with salt and pepper.

Bruschetta with Zucchini Puree

One day, I was sautéing some zucchini for a batch of Sautéed Zucchini with Caramelized Onions (page 119), and I suddenly found myself distracted. I returned to the stove to find that the zucchini were over-cooked. So I decided to make the best of it and stewed them to the point where they broke down. I then seasoned them up and made a spread. Well, the result was something a lot like this, and I think you'll agree that it makes an awesome bruschetta!

Serves 4-6

2 Tablespoons olive oil

1 large onion – finely diced

3 small zucchini – thinly sliced

2 cloves garlic – minced

2 Tablespoons chopped fresh flat leaf parsley

10 fresh basil leaves – chopped

1 Tablespoon chopped fresh oregano

Kosher salt

Freshly ground black pepper

8 thick slices good quality Italian bread

2 Tablespoons extra virgin olive oil

2 Tablespoons chopped hazelnuts or walnuts – toasted (optional)

- Preheat a grill or your oven's broiler.
- Heat olive oil in a large skillet gently over medium heat. Add onions and sauté until translucent.
- Add zucchini, garlic, parsley, basil, and oregano. Cover the pan and cook over low heat, stirring occasionally, until zucchini is very soft and breaks apart when stirred, about 15 minutes. Stir mixture thoroughly to make a "puree" in the pan. Season to taste with salt and pepper.
- While zucchini is cooking, brush bread slices with extra virgin olive oil, and grill or broil on just one side until nicely browned.
- Divide zucchini puree among bread slices and garnish with hazelnuts if using. Serve warm or at room temperature.

Bruschetta with Cannellini Beans and Crispy Prosciutto

The combination of flavors in this dish reminds me of some of my favorite Mexican dishes; however, it is the sweet red wine vinegar reduction and oven-roasted prosciutto on this bruschetta that makes it distinctly Italian and unbelievably popular every time I serve it.

Serves 6-8

7 Tablespoons extra virgin olive oil – divided

½ medium onion – finely diced

2 cloves garlic – minced

1 (16-ounce) can cannellini beans – drained but not rinsed (or 2 cups cooked white beans)

Kosher salt

Freshly ground white pepper

½ cup red wine vinegar

3 Tablespoons sugar

2 bay leaves

1 teaspoon juniper berries – crushed lightly

1 teaspoon black peppercorns

14 thick slices good quality Italian bread

½ recipe Oven-Roasted Prosciutto (page 183)

1 Tablespoon chopped fresh parsley (optional)

- Preheat a grill or your oven's broiler.

- Heat 2 Tablespoons olive oil in a skillet over medium heat. Add onions and garlic; cover and cook until onions are soft and translucent.

- Add beans to skillet with onions and garlic. Add salt to taste, cover, and cook until beans are heated through, about 8 minutes.

- Transfer mixture to a large bowl. Using a potato masher, mash the beans into the desired consistency. (I prefer mine to still be a tad chunky.) Season to taste with salt and white pepper. Set aside to cool to room temperature.

- While the mixture is cooling, combine vinegar, sugar, bay leaves, juniper berries, and peppercorns in a small saucepan. Over medium heat, reduce to about ¼ cup. Strain reduction and set aside to cool. Discard solids.

- When the bean mixture is at room temperature, stir in 3 Tablespoons olive oil to make mixture into a moist paste. Taste and adjust seasoning again.

- Brush bread slices with remaining 2 Tablespoons olive oil; grill or broil on just one side until nicely browned.

- Top bread with white bean puree and garnish with Oven Roasted Prosciutto.

- Drizzle red wine vinegar reduction on bruschetta, and top with fresh parsley, if using.

Bruschetta with Figs, Prosciutto, Radicchio, and Balsamic

This is a colorful and tasty dish. Be sure to keep it as rustic-looking as possible, and you will be rewarded with an antipasto that is show-stopping for its look and flavors!

Serves 6-8

1 small head radicchio – rinsed and dried

24 fresh black mission figs

14 slices prosciutto

16 thick slices good quality Italian bread

2 Tablespoons extra virgin olive oil

Balsamic Reduction (page 182) for drizzling

10 fresh basil leaves – roughly chopped (optional)

- Preheat a grill or your oven's broiler.
- Clean radicchio by removing outer leaves. Slice radicchio in half, place cut-side down on cutting board, and slice into thin semicircles. Transfer to small bowl and set aside.
- Cut figs lengthwise into quarters; set aside.
- Shred prosciutto slices by hand so that you have pieces of varying sizes and shapes, but all small enough to be eaten in one bite. Set aside.
- Brush bread slices with olive oil, and grill or broil on just one side until nicely browned.
- Top bruschetta with prosciutto, then figs, then radicchio. Drizzle balsamic reduction on all the slices and garnish with basil, if using.

Bruschetta with Baby Artichokes and Anchovies

To make this recipe come together quickly, use jarred marinated artichoke hearts. They are already cooked and in a vinaigrette, so you only need to whisk in chopped anchovies. Cooking your own baby artichokes and making your own dressing, however, creates a dish that is far superior.

Serves 4

4 baby artichokes – preferably with small stems still attached

Zest and juice of 1 lemon

2 Tablespoons olive oil

2 Tablespoons dry white wine

1 clove garlic – minced

1 shallot – minced

1 teaspoon fresh thyme leaves

1 Tablespoon white wine vinegar

3 anchovy fillets – minced super-fine

5 Tablespoons extra virgin olive oil – divided

Kosher salt

Freshly ground black pepper

8 thick slices good quality Italian bread

2 Tablespoons roughly chopped fresh flat leaf parsley

- Preheat a grill or your oven's broiler.
- Remove outer leaves of artichokes down to just the light colored internal leaves. Slice in half lengthwise (through the stem as well) and scoop out the hairy choke from inside the artichoke. Peel the skin from the stem of artichokes and place the artichokes in a bowl large enough to hold all four. Add water to cover and stir in lemon juice.
- Heat olive oil in a large skillet over medium-high heat. Cook the artichokes, cut-side down, until lightly browned. If you need to do this in batches, set cooked ones aside, add fresh olive oil and repeat until all are browned on the cut side. With all of the artichokes back in the skillet, add white wine, cover, and cook over medium heat until the hearts are tender, about 5 to 10 minutes.
- While the artichokes are cooking, make a vinaigrette by mixing the garlic, shallots, thyme, vinegar, and anchovies in a bowl. Gradually whisk in 3 Tablespoons extra virgin olive oil to emulsify. Season vinaigrette to taste with salt and pepper.

- Brush bread slices with remaining 2 Tablespoons extra virgin olive oil. Grill or broil on just one side until nicely browned.
- Top each bruschetta with one of the artichoke halves. Pour on some of the vinaigrette, and garnish with lemon zest and parsley.

FRITTATAS FOR ALL SEASONS

Frittatas are a cross between French omelets and American scrambled eggs. They straddle the line between comforting peasant food and classy cuisine. Last night's leftovers can be eaten as a breakfast, or can be sliced into small squares for a passed *anitpasto*. The beauty of a frittata is that it can be made with only the merest of additions to the egg base. To demonstrate their incredible versatility, I present a frittata recipe that matches each of the four seasons, so you can have fresh, seasonal frittatas all year long. Don't let these recipes be the end of your explorations! Really get creative with your next visit to the farmers market!

SPRING FRITTATA

Serves 4-6

½ pound thin asparagus – ends snapped

 cup fresh peas

8 large eggs

2 Tablespoons heavy cream

¾ ounces freshly grated *Parmigiano Reggiano* – plus more for garnish

½ teaspoon kosher salt

Pinch freshly ground black pepper

1 Tablespoon olive oil

2 cloves garlic – minced

4 ounces marinated artichokes (or 1 steamed artichoke, heart only – page 181) – cut into 1-inch pieces

1 Tablespoon chopped fresh tarragon

1 teaspoon Dijon mustard

Fresh arugula – rinsed and dried, for garnish

- Preheat the oven to 400° F.
- Prepare an ice bath by filling a large bowl with ice cubes and cold water. Set aside.
- In a large saucepan, over high heat, bring 6 cups water plus a healthy dash of salt to a boil. Add asparagus spears to water and blanch until tender, about 3 minutes. Remove asparagus from the water and place in the ice bath to stop the cooking. Blanch the peas in the same water until tender, then add them to the ice bath. Drain water from vegetables, pat dry, and set aside.
- In a large bowl, beat together eggs, cream, Parmesan, salt, and pepper.

- In a large ovenproof skillet, heat the olive oil over medium-high heat. Add asparagus and peas, and sauté until just beginning to color, about 3 minutes. Add garlic and artichokes, and sauté for 1 minute more.

- Reduce heat to medium. Pour in the egg mixture; and while it is wet, stir in the tarragon and mustard.

- Scramble the eggs lightly in the pan until they are about half cooked and somewhat set.

- Place frittata in oven and bake until frittata is completely cooked, about 5 to 10 minutes.

- Remove frittata from oven, garnish with extra Parmesan and arugula, and serve.

Summer Frittata

Serves 4-6

1 ear fresh corn – yellow or white

8 large eggs

2 Tablespoons heavy cream

¾ ounces freshly grated *Parmigiano Reggiano* – plus more for garnish

½ teaspoon kosher salt

Pinch freshly ground black pepper

1 Tablespoon olive oil

2 medium shallots – thinly sliced

1 zucchini – sliced into thin rounds

2 cloves garlic – minced

3 Tablespoons thinly sliced fresh basil – plus extra whole leaves for garnish

- Preheat oven to 400° F.
- In a medium saucepan over high heat, bring 4 cups water plus a healthy dash of salt to a boil.
- Slice the kernels from the corn cob, add them to water and cook until tender, about 4 minutes. Drain and rinse under cold water to stop the cooking. Set aside.
- In a large bowl, beat together eggs, cream, Parmesan, salt, and pepper to taste.
- In a large ovenproof skillet, heat olive oil over medium heat. Add shallots and cook slowly until shallots are nicely browned and caramelized, about 8 to 10 minutes.
- Mix in zucchini and garlic, and cook until zucchini is soft, about 5 more minutes.
- Stir in corn and basil, and sauté for 1 minute.
- Pour in the egg mixture and scramble lightly in the pan until eggs are about half cooked and somewhat set.
- Place frittata in oven and bake until frittata is completely cooked, about 5 to 10 minutes.
- Remove frittata from oven, garnish with extra Parmesan and basil, and serve.

Autumn Frittata

4 ounces rapini – rinsed, dried, and coarsely chopped

8 large eggs

2 Tablespoons heavy cream

¾ ounces freshly grated *Parmigiano Reggiano*

½ teaspoon kosher salt

Pinch freshly ground black pepper

¼ teaspoon crushed red pepper

1 Tablespoon olive oil

1 small leek – white and light green parts, thinly sliced

3 cloves garlic – minced

¼ cup Oven-Roasted Prosciutto (page 183)

½-1 teaspoon white truffle oil – for garnish

Fresh fennel fronds – for garnish

- Preheat oven to 400° F.
- In a medium saucepan over high heat, bring 4 cups water to a boil with a healthy dash of salt. Add rapini to saucepan and cook until tender, about 5 minutes. Drain, rinse under cold water, and press out excess water.
- In a large bowl, beat together eggs, cream, Parmesan, salt, black pepper to taste, and red pepper.
- In a large ovenproof skillet, heat olive oil over medium-high heat, and sauté the leeks and garlic until leeks are soft, about 3 minutes.
- Add rapini and sauté for 3 more minutes.
- Pour in the egg mixture, and add prosciutto. Scramble eggs lightly in the pan until they are about half cooked and somewhat set.
- Place frittata in oven and bake until frittata is completely cooked, about 5 to 10 minutes.
- Remove frittata from oven, garnish with white truffle oil and fennel fronds, and serve.

Winter Frittata

8 large eggs

2 Tablespoons heavy cream

¾ ounces freshly grated *Parmigiano Reggiano* – plus more for garnish

½ teaspoon kosher salt

Pinch freshly ground black pepper

1 Tablespoon olive oil

3 ounces pancetta – cut into 1-inch pieces

½ head radicchio – rinsed, dried, and thinly sliced (preferably on a mandoline), divided

¼ pound Brussels sprouts – thinly sliced (preferably on a mandoline)

3 ounces cooked shelled chestnuts – coarsely chopped

2 ounces goat cheese

- Preheat oven to 400° F.
- In a large bowl, beat together eggs, cream, Parmesan, salt, and pepper to taste.
- In a large ovenproof skillet, heat olive oil over medium-high heat, and sauté pancetta until crispy. Set aside ¼ cup of the sliced radicchio for garnish. Add Brussels sprouts and remaining radicchio, and sauté until both are nicely browned, about 3 to 5 minutes.
- Add chestnuts and sauté to heat through.
- Pour in the egg mixture, add goat cheese, and scramble eggs lightly in the pan until they are about half cooked and somewhat set.
- Place frittata in oven and bake until frittata is completely cooked, about 5 to 10 minutes.
- Remove frittata from oven, garnish with extra Parmesan and reserved radicchio, and serve.

Roasted Cremini Mushrooms Stuffed with Garlic and Parsley

I'm usually appalled by what people try to pass off as stuffed mushroom caps. Heavy fillings of sausage and cheese that are then allowed to get cold – why not just serve balls of fat? The simple ingredients here will surprise your guests, as the flavors will truly explode in their mouths. Best of all, you can actually *taste* the mushrooms in this recipe. Select the mushrooms individually; don't just buy a packaged collection. You'll need the best ones to make this dish work. Have some good bread on hand to sop up any juices that are left behind.

Serves 4-6

16-20 cremini mushrooms – good quality, about 2 inches in diameter

Good quality extra virgin olive oil

2 cloves garlic – thinly sliced

16-20 fresh flat leaf parsley leaves – roughly chopped

Kosher salt

Freshly ground black pepper

- Preheat oven to 425° F. Line a baking sheet with parchment paper.
- Clean out mushrooms with a spoon to remove all of the stems and any dark gills. You really want just the caps for this recipe.
- Place caps on prepared baking sheet.
- Pour olive oil into each of the mushroom caps – creating a little puddle of oil in each cap.
- Divide garlic and parsley evenly among the caps.
- Season mushrooms to taste with salt and pepper, and dot with a little more olive oil on top.
- Roast mushroom caps until mushrooms begin to brown around the edges, and begin to release their water, about 10 minutes.
- Transfer to small plates and serve while still hot.

Note: These caps will be full of juice in both the form of the olive oil and the mushroom water, which can pour out when they are bitten into. I like to use mushroom caps that are bite-size to avoid any dripping mishaps. And be careful, this juice is likely to be hot!

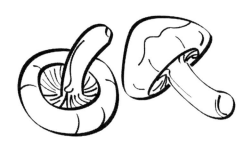

BROILED STUFFED CLAMS

Very similar to Clams Casino, this recipe is the lighter, more healthful version of that classic. Of course, if you want to sauté a little pancetta or *guanciale* and incorporate that into this recipe, I'm not going to tell anyone…

Serves 4-6

24 littleneck clams

2 cups dry white wine

3 bay leaves

1 Tablespoon whole black peppercorns

1 Tablespoon whole coriander seeds

2 Tablespoons finely chopped fresh flat leaf parsley

2 cloves garlic – minced

¼ cup extra virgin olive oil – plus more for drizzling

½ cup fresh breadcrumbs

Kosher salt

Freshly ground black pepper

Lemon wedges (optional)

- Wash and scrub clams to remove any dirt from the outside. Discard any clams that don't clamp shut firmly when handled as they are probably dead.
- In a large saucepot, combine wine, bay leaves, peppercorns, and coriander seeds. Bring to a light boil.
- Add clams and cook, covered, until clam shells pop open. The times will vary, so start checking after a minute or two. As soon as a clam opens, remove it from the pot to a plate. When all the clams are out, let them cool until you can handle them.
- Remove the clam flesh from the shell. Reserve the half of the shell that the clam flesh was attached to; discard the other half.
- In a small bowl, mix together parsley, garlic, olive oil, and breadcrumbs. Season to taste with salt and pepper.
- Preheat your broiler. While it is heating, return the clam flesh to the reserved shell pieces, and top each with some of the breadcrumb mixture. Drizzle a little more olive oil over each of the clams, and broil until the breadcrumbs form a nice golden crust, about 1 to 3 minutes.
- Serve immediately, while hot, with some lemon wedges on the side, if you like.

ROASTED PEPPERS WITH ANCHOVIES

The bright colors and rich, salty flavors of this *antipasto* make it a great choice to serve before large meals. It's very important that you make this well ahead of time, as the flavors need a chance to blend together.

Serves 4-6

3 bell peppers (red, yellow, or orange, or any mixture of these three)

1 Tablespoon butter

1 shallot – thinly sliced

5 anchovy fillets

1 Tablespoon finely chopped fresh oregano – divided

2 cloves garlic – minced

1 Tablespoon capers – drained, rinsed, and minced

1 Tablespoon red wine vinegar

¼ cup extra virgin olive oil

Kosher salt

Freshly ground black pepper

1 Tablespoon chopped fresh flat leaf parsley

- Preheat oven to 400° F. Line a rimmed baking sheet with parchment paper.
- Cut peppers in half lengthwise, remove all ribs and seeds.
- Cut each half pepper lengthwise into thirds, giving you strips about 2 inches wide.
- Bake peppers on the prepared baking sheet for 20 minutes. Remove and let cool.
- While the peppers are baking, melt butter in a small saucepan over medium heat, and sauté shallots until soft and lightly golden, about 10 minutes. Set aside.
- Dry anchovies on paper towels, remove any large bones, and cut into small pieces.
- In a small bowl, mix together shallots, anchovies, oregano, garlic, capers, vinegar, and olive oil. Set aside until peppers are cool.
- Drizzle the oil mixture evenly over the peppers.
- Cover peppers loosely with plastic wrap, and let stand at least 2 hours (up to 6) to allow flavors to come together.
- Remove plastic wrap, season to taste with salt and pepper, and garnish with parsley.

BAGNA CAUDA

This recipe literally means "hot bath" and it is meant for bathing vegetables. It is pretty much used like a fondue – different foods are dipped in and eaten. The simplicity of the preparation means it can be enjoyed at any time. It is especially good with artichoke leaves.

Serves 4-8

¾ cup extra virgin olive oil

4 Tablespoons unsalted butter – softened and cut into 4 pieces

10 anchovy fillets (about 2 ounces)

6 cloves garlic

Kosher salt

Freshly ground black pepper

Crusty bread, torn into bite-size pieces

Assorted raw and/or cooked vegetables

- Place olive oil, butter, anchovies, garlic, and salt and pepper to taste in a blender or food processor. Blend until smooth.
- Scrape out mixture into a small saucepan and bring to a simmer over medium heat.
- Reduce heat to low and cook, stirring occasionally, for about 20 minutes, or until the bubbling subsides. (Sauce will separate.)
- Strain bagna cauda into a fondue pot or other flameproof dish. Serve over a low open flame to keep sauce warm while dipping in pieces of crusty bread and vegetables.

Insalata

The Italian tradition of salads ranges from separate *antipasti*, to side dishes, to great ways of using leftovers for lunch the next day. While an *Insalata Caprese* (tomato, basil and fresh mozzarella) is one of the best known – and best loved – Italian salads, there are many more that can be enjoyed without the use of tomatoes.

Salads in Italian cooking are used in two ways: the refreshing small salad that begins or ends a meal and the large salad that is the meal itself. I like to think that any of these salad recipes can be used in either fashion.

Without question, this is the time to take care to purchase the freshest ingredients since there is nothing less attractive than a salad made with wilted dirty greens topped with a dressing full of dried herbs. Best ingredients in means fabulous salad out. When was the last time your salad stole the show at a meal?

INSALATA MISTA

There is no other way to think of this salad than as a "mixed salad," but please don't go out and buy the bag of "Italian Greens" you find at your local supermarket! Take the time to purchase fresh heads of Boston Bibb lettuce and wild arugula. Inspect the frisée and escarole for freshness and color. And don't you dare drown these greens in a bottle of whatever is passing as "Italian Dressing" in the cavernous aisles of the grocery store. Light, refreshing, simple dressings that just coat the greens are the name of the game, people! More likely than not, you'll surprise yourself.

Serves 4-6

4 cups mixed fresh greens (Examples: romaine, Boston Bibb, arugula, escarole, frisée, radicchio, mache) – rinsed and dried

1 small carrot – peeled and thinly sliced

½ small fennel bulb – thinly sliced

½ small cucumber – thinly sliced

Kosher salt

Freshly ground black pepper

2 Tablespoons red wine vinegar or fresh lemon juice

2 teaspoons fresh herbs (Examples: oregano, basil, thyme, tarragon) – minced

1 small clove garlic – minced

⅓ cup extra virgin olive oil

- Combine greens in a large salad bowl, and give them a toss to make sure they are well mixed.
- Add carrots, fennel, and cucumbers to the salad, and toss lightly again to combine.
- Season salad lightly with salt and pepper, and toss again.
- In a small bowl, whisk together vinegar, fresh herbs, and garlic. Stir in a pinch of salt and pepper.
- While whisking, slowly add olive oil to the vinegar mixture to make a well-emulsified vinaigrette.
- Right before serving, pour the dressing over the salad, and toss to combine one last time. Serve, making sure every plate has a nice mix of all the salad ingredients.

Bean and Tuna Salad with White Balsamic Vinegar

Plain old tuna salad takes a great Italian twist here with the addition of white beans. The brightness of white balsamic vinegar makes the whole dish come alive. This can easily be served as a side salad with almost any springtime meal, as a picnic lunch, or as an appetizer served on thick slices of Italian or French bread. White balsamic vinegar can be hard to come by, but it is well worth the search! Regular balsamic would turn the salad gray and unattractive. Use white balsamic if you can get your hands on it, but use white wine vinegar if you can't.

Serves 4-6

1 (15-ounce) can cannellini beans – drained and rinsed

1 (5-ounce) can tuna – drained and flaked

¼ cup red onion – finely diced

2 cloves garlic – minced

3 Tablespoons chopped fresh flat leaf parsley

2 Tablespoons chopped fresh oregano

3 Tablespoons white balsamic vinegar

1 Tablespoon extra virgin olive oil

Kosher salt

Freshly ground black pepper

- Combine beans, tuna, onion, garlic, parsley, and oregano in a bowl.
- Add vinegar and then olive oil. If salad is too dry, add a little more of each to balance the overall flavoring in the salad, and reach the desired consistency.
- Season to taste with salt and pepper.

Mixed Bean Salad with Pesto and Asparagus

This salad combines so many flavors and colors – it's a sure to become a favorite side dish at any picnic. With the addition of the pesto, there is no need for extra cheese, oil, or herbs; they're already all in there! It's a snap to quickly bring this salad together for a lazy afternoon lunch in the summer.

Serves 4-6

1 (15-ounce) can cannellini beans, drained but not rinsed

1 (15-ounce) can black beans, drained but not rinsed

1 (15-ounce) can kidney beans, drained but not rinsed

½ pound asparagus

¼ cup Fresh Pesto (page 55)

¼ cup Peperonata (page 180) – coarsely chopped

3 ounces goat cheese – crumbled

¼ cup Kalamata olives – pitted and sliced

1 small shallot – minced

Kosher salt

Freshly ground black pepper

- Bring a large pot of salted water to a boil
- Place all beans in a large bowl.
- Snap the tough ends off the asparagus spears and slice spears on the diagonal into 3-inch lengths. Add asparagus to boiling water and simmer until tender, about 4 minutes. Drain, and rinse with cold water. Add asparagus to beans.
- Add the Fresh Pesto, Peperonata, cheese, olives, and, shallots. Toss gently to combine.
- Season to taste with salt and pepper.

PANZANELLA OF BELL PEPPERS

This salad is one that usually has tomatoes, but the real heart of this salad is the bread, hence the use of *pane*, meaning "bread," in the name. The best choice is leftover stale bread which will soak up the flavors of the oil, vinegar, and fresh herbs very well. Although it is traditional to for Tuscan bread to be made without salt, I prefer to make it with salt. Use leftover Focaccia (page 176) to make this salad extra wonderful.

Serves 4-6

6 Tablespoons red wine vinegar

1 clove garlic – minced

1 teaspoon minced fresh thyme

1 teaspoon minced fresh oregano

¼ teaspoon crushed red pepper

½ teaspoon kosher salt

¼ teaspoon freshly ground black pepper

¾ cup extra virgin olive oil

3 cups stale bread cubes (or lightly toasted fresh bread cubes)

2 red bell peppers

1 yellow (or orange) bell pepper

1 green bell pepper

¼ red onion

1 large cucumber

½ pound fresh mozzarella

20-30 large fresh basil leaves – roughly torn by hand

- In a medium bowl, whisk together vinegar, garlic, thyme, oregano, red pepper, salt, and black pepper. While continuing to whisk, slowly add olive oil to the bowl, and whisk to fully emulsify.
- Pour half of the vinaigrette into a large serving bowl and set aside. Add bread cubes to the remaining vinaigrette in the medium bowl, and toss to coat. Set aside to soak while you make the rest of the salad.
- Remove seeds and ribs from all peppers; and cut peppers into 1-inch squares. Toss with the vinaigrette in the large serving bowl.
- Cut onion into thin slices; toss with peppers.
- Peel cucumber and slice in half lengthwise. Using a spoon, remove and discard the seeds. Slice cucumber crosswise into semicircles. Toss with peppers and onions.
- Cut mozzarella into ½-inch cubes and toss with peppers.

- Add the bread cubes to the salad, making sure to include any vinaigrette that did not get absorbed, and toss everything together to combine. Taste and adjust seasoning.
- Top the salad with basil leaves and toss lightly. Serve immediately.

Radicchio, Endive, and Arugula Salad with Blood Orange Vinaigrette

This recipe combines flavor elements from two salads I made at one of the restaurants I worked in. Each salad was okay on its own, but I saw the potential in combining them. With the beloved blood oranges of Sicily, this makes for a truly Italian-inspired salad.

Serves 4-6

For the Salad:

1 head radicchio lettuce – cored, quartered, and leaves separated, rinsed and dried

2 medium Belgium endives – leaves separated rinsed and dried

2 cups arugula – rinsed and dried

For the Vinaigrette:

Juice and zest of 1 blood orange

½ small shallot – minced

1 teaspoon finely chopped fresh basil

1 teaspoon red wine vinegar

1 Tablespoon extra virgin olive oil

5 Tablespoons vegetable oil

Kosher salt

Freshly ground black pepper

Finishing Touches:

4 ounces good quality goat cheese – coarsely crumbled

¾ ounces pistachios – roasted and coarsely chopped

2 blood oranges – peeled, individual segments removed from their membranes

- Place all greens together in a large bowl.
- Strain orange juice into a small bowl; add zest, shallots, basil, and vinegar. Slowly whisk in olive oil and then vegetable oil to emulsify. Season vinaigrette to taste with salt and pepper.
- When ready to serve, toss lettuces with dressing. Season to taste with salt and pepper.
- Divide among four to six salad plates and top evenly with goat cheese, pistachios, and blood orange segments.

Zuppa

The degree to which chefs are capable of waxing poetic about soup knows no bounds. But I can understand where they're coming from. It's so incredibly comforting to have a steaming bowl of soup in front of you that it warms you instantly and thoroughly. How can you not fall in love with soup?

In Italian cooking, soups definitely come from the tradition of *cucina povera*, the food of the poor people. It's one-pot cooking at its best. The collection of ingredients is based on what is available; or, in many cases, what is left over from the previous day's meal.

But that doesn't mean Italian *zuppa* is just a hodgepodge of random scraps thrown together with water or stock in a pot and heated through. There is real cooking to be done here, and amazing flavors to elicit from the ingredients. Because the soups are based on what is available at the time, they instantly lend themselves to cooking with only the freshest local and seasonal ingredients. If that's not what Italian cooking is all about, then I don't know what is.

MINESTRONE

There are as many different recipes for minestrone as there are grandmothers in Italy. No one recipe can claim to be "the one true minestrone." But beans, vegetables, and pasta almost always make an appearance. I throw in a little of my Fresh Pesto for flavor; but if you just want to use fresh basil leaves, the result is just as great.

Serves 4-6

¼ cup olive oil

¼ cup diced pancetta (or bacon)

2 small onions – diced

2 carrots – peeled and diced

2 stalks celery – diced

5 cloves garlic – minced

3 Tablespoons Fresh Pesto (page 55)

1 (15-ounce) can red kidney beans – drained but not rinsed

7 cups Chicken Stock (page 173)

½ pound pasta – penne, orecchiette, or other "short" cut pasta

Kosher salt

Freshly ground black pepper

Freshly grated *Parmigiano Reggiano* – for garnish

Chopped fresh parsley – for garnish

- Line a plate with paper towels.
- Heat olive oil in a large heavy soup pot over medium heat.
- Add pancetta and cook until crisp. Remove with slotted spoon to the lined plate.
- Add onions, carrots, and celery to olive oil; cook until onion is translucent.
- Add garlic; cook until fragrant, about 30 seconds.
- Return the pancetta to the pot and add Fresh Pesto, beans, and Chicken Stock. Using a spoon, scrape up all the browned bits from the bottom of the pot.
- Bring soup to a boil, and then add pasta. Cook until pasta is *al dente*. Season to taste with salt and pepper.
- Serve soup immediately, garnished with Parmesan and parsley.

Summer Vegetable Soup from Umbria

When making Minestrone (page 33), you must cook the vegetables for a long time to really soften them, and merge all of their flavors into one rich uniform soup. The only thing in it that cooks briefly is the pasta. By contrast, in this soup, everything cooks quickly to preserve their individual textures and flavors, but they still combine together beautifully!

Serves 4-6

2 Tablespoons extra virgin olive oil

2 shallots – minced

2 cloves garlic – minced

10 fresh basil leaves – minced

1 Tablespoon minced fresh flat leaf parsley

2 stalks celery – thinly sliced

1 carrot – peeled and thinly sliced

2 cups Chicken Stock (page 173)

2 cups hot water

2 teaspoons salt

1 yellow squash – halved, seeded and cut into ¾-inch cubes

¼ pound red potatoes – unpeeled, scrubbed, and cut into ½-inch cubes

1 cup coarsely chopped Swiss chard leaves – rinsed and dried, stems discarded (about 2 ounces)

½ cup fresh or frozen green peas

¼ pound thin asparagus – cut into 1-inch pieces

Kosher salt

Freshly ground black pepper

Freshly grated *Parmigiano Reggiano* – for garnish

- In a large saucepan, over medium heat, heat olive oil until shimmering. Add shallots, and cook until translucent. Add garlic, basil and parsley, and cook until fragrant, about 1 more minute.
- Add celery and carrots. Increase heat to medium-high and cook until vegetables begin to get some color, about 5 minutes.
- Add Chicken Stock, water, and salt; bring to a boil. Reduce heat to a simmer and cook until vegetables are tender, about 10 minutes.
- Add squash and potatoes, and simmer for 5 minutes.

- Add chard, peas, and asparagus. Simmer for about 5 more minutes, or until all the vegetables are tender.
- Season soup to taste with salt and pepper, and serve with Parmesan.

CHICKPEA SOUP

There are a lot of soups in Italy, and it is the chickpea soups that most define the central states. You can use dried chickpeas (garbanzos) in this recipe, but that involves overnight soaking and extra cooking time, so I'm using the canned chickpeas to save you some time. They're easy to find, and you can make this soup quickly as a result.

Serves 4-6

3 Tablespoons olive oil

1 onion – diced

2 stalks celery – diced

1 large carrot – peeled and diced

3 cloves garlic – minced

3 sprigs fresh rosemary

3 sprigs fresh thyme

2 bay leaves

2 (15-ounce) cans chickpeas – drained and rinsed

½ cup dry white wine

3 cups Chicken Stock (page 173)

1 cup hot water

Kosher salt

Freshly ground black pepper

Crushed red pepper

Freshly grated *Parmigiano Reggiano* – for garnish

1-2 Tablespoons extra virgin olive oil – for garnish

<u>Special equipment needed</u>: 100% cotton cheesecloth and kitchen twine

- In a large soup pot, heat olive oil over medium heat. Add onions and sauté until translucent.
- Add celery, carrots, and garlic. Cook for an additional 5 minutes, until carrots soften slightly.
- Tie together rosemary sprigs, thyme sprigs, and bay leaves in the cheesecloth and secure with kitchen twine to create an herb sachet.
- Add the herb sachet, chickpeas, and wine; cook for 5 minutes.
- Add Chicken Stock and water, and bring to a boil. Reduce heat to a simmer. Cook until chickpeas are heated through and tender, about 20 minutes. Remove and discard the herb sachet.
- Season to taste with salt, pepper, and red pepper.
- Serve hot with Parmesan and a drizzle of extra virgin olive oil.

POLENTA AND KALE SOUP

This is not a recipe for making polenta – that dish has its own chapter later in this book. This soup makes use of the coarse-ground cornmeal, though, for texture and flavor. Feel free to change the greens in this soup. Collard greens, spinach, or the traditional *cavolo nero* (black cabbage) are all great substitutes for the kale.

Serves 4-6

4 Tablespoons extra virgin olive oil – divided, plus extra for garnish

2 shallots – minced

3 cloves garlic – minced

3-3½ cups Chicken Stock (page 173)

3 cups hot water

3 sprigs fresh thyme

3 bay leaves

Zest of 1 lemon

½ cup polenta (coarse ground cornmeal)

2 teaspoons kosher salt

½ cup freshly grated *Parmigiano Reggiano*

3 cups coarsely chopped kale leaves

½ teaspoon freshly grated nutmeg

Freshly ground black pepper

Special equipment needed: 100% cotton cheesecloth and kitchen twine

- Heat 2 Tablespoons olive oil in a large saucepan over medium heat. Add shallots and garlic, and sauté until shallots are translucent, being careful not to let the garlic burn, about 3 minutes.
- Add Chicken Stock and water. Increase heat to medium-high; bring to a boil.
- While soup is coming to a boil, tie together thyme, bay leaves, and lemon zest in the cheesecloth and secure with kitchen twine to create an herb sachet. Add herb sachet to the soup.
- When the soup comes to a boil, slowly add polenta in a steady stream while continually whisking. Add salt and stir to combine.
- Reduce heat to medium and simmer, stirring occasionally, for 15 minutes to allow mixture to thicken slightly.
- Stir in Parmesan and remaining 2 Tablespoons olive oil. Remove and discard the herb sachet.
- Add kale and nutmeg, and cook until kale wilts slightly, about 2 minutes.
- Garnish soup with extra virgin olive oil and freshly ground black pepper. Serve immediately.

Borlotti Bean Soup with Sautéed Escarole

Borlotti beans are a staple of Northern Italy because they are loaded with protein and minerals. A bowl of this soup is both comforting and very good for you! You can, of course, use dried beans; just be sure to soak them overnight and add an extra cup of water in the cooking process. You'll need about 2 cups of dried beans for this recipe. I use the canned beans here to help make things go faster for you. In the United States, borlotti beans are more commonly called cranberry beans.

Serves 4-6

5 Tablespoons olive oil – divided, plus more oil for drizzling

1 onion – diced

4 cloves garlic – minced, divided

1 carrot – peeled and diced

1 stalk celery – diced

½ cup dry white wine

2 bay leaves

¼ cup fresh flat leaf parsley leaves

3 sprigs fresh oregano

2 (15-ounce) cans borlotti (cranberry) beans – drained but not rinsed

3-3½ cups Chicken Stock (page 173)

1 head escarole –white ends trimmed, leaves coarsely torn, rinsed and dried

Kosher salt

Freshly ground black pepper

Special equipment needed: 100% cotton cheesecloth and kitchen twine

- Heat 2 Tablespoons olive oil in a large saucepan over medium-high heat. Add onions and 3 cloves garlic. Sauté until the onions are translucent.
- Add carrots and celery; mix well. Reduce heat to medium and cook until the vegetables are tender, about 3 minutes.
- Add wine and deglaze the pan by cooking, stirring to scrape up all the browned bits on the bottom of the pan, until almost all the wine is gone.
- While the wine is simmering, tie together bay leaves, parsley, and oregano in the cheesecloth and secure with kitchen twine to create an herb sachet.
- Add this herb sachet and beans to the pot with enough Chicken Stock to cover the beans by about 1 inch.
- Bring to a simmer, and continue to gently simmer soup for 15 minutes.

- While soup is simmering, heat remaining 3 Tablespoons olive oil in a large skillet over medium heat. Add escarole and remaining 1 clove garlic. Sauté until escarole is tender and developing a little color. Season to taste with salt and pepper. Keep warm over low heat.

- When soup is done simmering, press out all the liquid from the herb sachet, and stir the liquid into the soup. Discard sachet.

- Run the soup through a food mill or puree in a blender to make the entire soup smooth and creamy. Return soup to cooking pot, and place the pot back over medium heat to warm through. If soup is too thin, cook down a little longer. If soup is too thick, add additional stock or water to thin it out.

- Season soup to taste with salt and pepper, and serve with sautéed escarole and a drizzle of extra virgin olive oil on top.

BUTTERNUT SQUASH SOUP GRATINATA

Gratinata is what we would commonly call "Au Gratin" here in the United States, but that's a French term, so let's use the Italian phrasing for this book. The concept, however, is the same. A lovely butternut squash soup is topped off with toasted Asiago cheese and Herbed Candied Walnuts for a perfect blending off flavors and textures.

Serves 4-6

3 pounds butternut squash (1 large or 2 small)

2 ounces pancetta – cut in small cubes

1 large shallot – minced

1 cup Chicken Stock (page 173)

3 cups hot water

Kosher salt

½ cup heavy cream

⅓ cup shredded Asiago

1 recipe Herbed Candied Walnuts (page 184)

- Line a plate with paper towels.
- Peel butternut squash and cut it in half lengthwise. Scoop out strings and seeds; place in a small bowl and set aside. Do not discard. Cut flesh of squash into large chunks. Place squash flesh into a steamer basket that fits over a large soup pot. Set aside.
- In the large soup pot over medium heat, sauté pancetta until crisp. Transfer to the lined plate.
- Add shallots to the rendered fat in the soup pot, and sauté until translucent. Add strings and seeds of the squash. Cook until fragrant and dark orange, about 5 minutes.
- Add Chicken Stock, water, and 1 teaspoon salt to the pot; bring to a boil.
- Place the steamer basket over the soup, reduce to a simmer, cover, and steam the squash until tender, about 30 minutes.
- While squash is steaming, preheat oven to 400° F.
- Remove squash flesh from steamer basket, and place in blender. Strain steaming liquid, reserving liquid and discarding solids. Add liquid to the flesh in the blender and carefully puree until smooth. (Do in batches if necessary.)
- Return soup to the pot, and stir in cream. Season to taste with salt.
- Divide soup among oven-safe soup bowls and sprinkle cooked pancetta and then Asiago over the soup. Place bowls on a baking sheet, place in the oven. Bake until the cheese melts, about 10 minutes.
- Remove soup from oven, garnish each bowl with Herbed Candied Walnuts and serve immediately.

Pizza

Can a good pizza really be made without using tomatoes? Call up your favorite pizza delivery place, and you'll find that the default pizza will be covered in a thick layer of below average red sauce. Sometimes you can find a place that may have a specialty pizza or two that doesn't involve tomatoes, but when people think pizza, tomatoes naturally spring to mind.

Arguably the greatest form of pizza – pizza margherita – has tomatoes on it as well. The people of Naples will tout their local San Marzanos as the best tomatoes suited to the task – and I'm inclined to agree. No, I won't be offering up a tomato-free version of this classic Italian pie just for the sake of squeezing such a popular pizza into this book. Pizza margherita is already perfect the way it is – if you want to use my pizza dough to make one for yourself, please go right ahead!

Just because we have been programmed to think of pizza as a vehicle for tomatoes doesn't mean that we can't turn that idea on its head. We'll still be making pizza, just not ones that follow the same old model of dough, tomato sauce, cheese, and toppings. Prepare to try something new!

You may never pick up the phone to order a pizza again…

CHEF MATT'S FAMOUS PIZZA DOUGH

If you're going to make pizza, you need a great pizza dough. The good news about pizza dough is that it's remarkably easy to make. The tough part is that there is one special ingredient that is relatively hard to come by: the flour.

"Tipo OO" flour is without a doubt the best for pizza dough. (In my opinion, The Molino Caputo family makes the best "OO" flour out there.) It is super-fine flour that produces a silky, flaky crust that is just superb, but the flour can be rather tough to track down. If you can't get your hands on it, use an American bread flour. You'll still get the best pizza crust you've ever had.

Makes 3 medium or 2 large pizza crusts

12½ ounces warm water

½ teaspoon sugar

1 packet dry active yeast (7 grams – ¼ ounce)

¼ teaspoon dried rosemary

¼ teaspoon dried oregano

¼ teaspoon dried basil

21 ounces (4½ cups) Tipo "OO" flour – or bread flour

5 teaspoons kosher salt

- Mix warm water, sugar, and yeast in a 2-cup measuring cup; stir until dissolved and cover with plastic wrap. Allow to proof for 10 minutes or so, until bubbles form on surface of the water.
- Place dried herbs in a spice grinder or mortar, and grind to break up large pieces (especially the dried rosemary.)
- In a large mixing bowl, mix flour, salt, and dried herbs with a spoon.
- Pour proofed yeast mixture into flour mixture, and stir to combine until the dough comes together.
- Pour dough out onto a clean, dry work surface (with no extra flour!), and knead until elastic, about 5 to 8 minutes. (Or place mixture in a Kitchen Aid with the dough hook attachment and mix on low speed for about 4 minutes, then remove to table and knead by hand for 1 more minute.)
- Place dough ball into a bowl rubbed with a light coat of olive oil, cover, and let sit to rise until doubled in size – about 1 to 1½ hours.
- Punch dough down, and divide it into thirds.
- Without kneading, shape dough into three balls, about 11 ounces each. Cover with a damp cloth, and let rise again at room temperature for 30 minutes. Or, if you want to use the dough later, you can let it rise in the fridge for up to 24 hours.

Note: If you want to make larger pizzas, divide the dough into only two balls; but you'll have to increase the amount of toppings for your pizzas in the following recipes.

ASPARAGUS PIZZA

Thin asparagus, which you don't have to peel, creates the best results for this pizza. They are tender, are a rich green color, and are the most flavorful. The mozzarella cheese is best if cubed; but if you can't find a block to cube up, shredded works fine.

Serves 2-3

1 Tbsp fine ground cornmeal

1 ball Pizza Dough (page 43)

½ pound thin asparagus

3 Tablespoons extra virgin olive oil – divided

1 (6-ounce) block mozzarella – cut into ½-inch cubes

2 cloves garlic – minced

¼ cup freshly grated *Parmigiano Reggiano*

Freshly ground black pepper

- Preheat oven to 500° F. If you have a pizza stone, make sure that it is well preheated in the oven as well. Sprinkle cornmeal on pizza peel if using a pizza stone, or if you don't have a pizza stone, sprinkle cornmeal on a round baking sheet. Set aside.

- Snap the tough ends off asparagus spears, and rinse the spears. Pat dry with paper towels, and set aside.

- Roll out one ball of Pizza Dough, place on pizza peel if using a pizza stone, or on the prepared round baking sheet if you're not. Brush with 1 Tablespoon olive oil.

- Lay asparagus spears across dough – not in any specific arrangement, just as they fall – and then scatter mozzarella and garlic among the spears.

- Using pizza peel, transfer pizza onto pizza stone, or simply place baking sheet with pizza into oven.

- Rotating the pizza a few times during baking to ensure even browning, bake pizza until crust is crisp and well-browned on all sides and the asparagus is nicely cooked as well, about 8 minutes.

- Remove pizza from oven, and drizzle remaining 2 Tablespoons olive oil on top. Sprinkle on Parmesan and season to taste with black pepper. Serve immediately.

PIZZA

Pizza with Artichokes, Roasted Red Peppers, and Goat Cheese

You can use steamed fresh artichokes (page 181) and roast your own red peppers (page 179) for this pizza if you like. But if you are already making dough from scratch, you may want to give yourself a break and use the jarred varieties of both of these vegetables to save yourself some time. Also, if you want to take a break from the theme of this cookbook, oil-soaked sun-dried tomatoes make a wonderful addition to this pizza.

Serves 2-3

1 Tbsp fine ground cornmeal

1 ball Pizza Dough (page 43)

2 Tablespoons extra virgin olive oil – divided

1–1½ cups shredded mozzarella

½ cup marinated artichoke hearts – cut into eighths

1 roasted red bell pepper – seeded and cut into thin strips

4 ounces goat cheese – crumbled

1 scallion – green part only, thinly sliced

Kosher salt

Freshly ground black pepper

- Preheat oven to 500° F. If you have a pizza stone, make sure that it is well preheated in the oven as well. Sprinkle cornmeal on pizza peel if using a pizza stone, or if you don't have a pizza stone, sprinkle cornmeal on a round baking sheet. Set aside.
- Roll out one ball of Pizza Dough, place on pizza peel if using a pizza stone, or on the prepared round baking sheet if you're not. Brush crust with 1 Tablespoon olive oil.
- Top pizza with mozzarella, artichokes, red peppers, and goat cheese.
- Using pizza peel, transfer pizza onto pizza stone, or simply place baking sheet with pizza into oven.
- Rotating the pizza a few times during baking to ensure even browning, bake pizza until crust is crisp and well-browned on all sides and the goat cheese is lightly browned as well, about 8 to 10 minutes total.
- Remove pizza from oven, top with scallions.
- Drizzle on remaining 1 Tablespoon olive oil, and season with salt and pepper to taste.
- Slice and serve immediately.

Pizza with Figs, Gorgonzola, Prosciutto, and Balsamic

This pizza is a creation of mine that combines some of my favorite flavors of autumn. Be sure to use rainbow chard, if you can, since it is a lovely final addition and a true autumn green to match the seasonality of the fresh figs. If you can't get your hands on chard, wild arugula makes a fine substitution. You must use fresh figs, however; soaked dried figs will not work on this pizza.

Serves 2-3

1 Tbsp fine ground cornmeal

1 ball Pizza Dough (page 43)

²⁄₃ cup shredded mozzarella

2 ounces Gorgonzola – crumbled

4 fresh black mission figs – quartered

2 ounces thinly sliced prosciutto – torn into rough strips

4-5 fresh rainbow chard leaves – rinsed and dried, stems removed, cut into long thin strips

1 Tablespoon Balsamic Reduction (page 182)

- Preheat oven to 500° F. If you have a pizza stone, make sure that it is well preheated in the oven as well. Sprinkle cornmeal on pizza peel if using a pizza stone, or if you don't have a pizza stone, sprinkle cornmeal on a round baking sheet. Set aside.

- Roll out one ball of Pizza Dough, place on pizza peel if using a pizza stone, or on the prepared round baking sheet if you're not. Top with mozzarella, Gorgonzola, and figs.

- Using pizza peel, transfer pizza onto pizza stone, or simply place baking sheet with pizza into oven.

- Rotating the pizza a few times during baking to ensure even browning, bake pizza until crust is crisp and well-browned on all sides and figs are beginning to "melt" into the cheese, about 8 minutes.

- Remove pizza from oven, top with prosciutto, rainbow chard, and Balsamic Reduction.

- Slice and serve immediately.

SUMMER SQUASH PIZZA WITH ONION AND RICOTTA SALATA

This pizza makes the most of summer in a way that is usually reserved for the ripest of tomatoes. In this instance, we add onions, fresh herbs, and the sharp, salty note of ricotta salata to the pizza. It will look different than anything you've ever made; but after one bite, you know you'll be making it again.

Serves 2-3

1 Tbsp fine ground cornmeal

2 Tablespoons olive oil – divided

1 onion – thinly sliced

1 ball Pizza Dough (page 43)

$\frac{2}{3}$ cup shredded mozzarella

1 teaspoon fresh oregano or marjoram leaves

1 teaspoon fresh thyme leaves

1 teaspoon fresh basil leaves

1 small zucchini – thinly sliced

1 small yellow squash - thinly sliced

½ cup freshly grated ricotta salata

- Preheat oven to 500° F. If you have a pizza stone, make sure that it is well preheated in the oven as well. Sprinkle cornmeal on pizza peel if using a pizza stone, or if you don't have a pizza stone, sprinkle cornmeal on a round baking sheet. Set aside.

- In a small skillet, heat 1 Tablespoon olive oil over medium-high heat. Add onions and sauté until soft and lightly golden in color.

- Roll out one ball of Pizza Dough, place on pizza peel if using a pizza stone, or on the prepared round baking sheet if you're not. Top dough with sautéed onions first.

- Top onions with shredded mozzarella, then herbs, and finally the sliced squash.

- Using pizza peel, transfer pizza onto pizza stone, or simply place baking sheet with pizza into oven.

- Rotating the pizza a few times during baking to ensure even browning, bake pizza until crust is crisp and well-browned on all sides and squash is browning lightly on top, about 8 to 10 minutes.

- Remove pizza from oven, and sprinkle ricotta salata all over the top.

- Slice and serve immediately.

WHITE PIZZA WITH ITALIAN SAUSAGE AND PESTO

The trick to a good white pizza is the blend of cheeses. I'm presenting my personal favorite here, but you can tweak the ratios of cheeses yourself to find what works best for you. Just make sure the result isn't too oily! I then top the pizza with some more toppings that really make the pizza stand out, but you can just leave it as a plain white if you like.

Serves 2-3

1 Tbsp fine ground cornmeal

1 ball Pizza Dough (page 43)

⅓ cup fresh whole milk ricotta – dried on paper towels for 20 minutes

½ cup shredded mozzarella

½ cup shredded asiago

¼ cup grated *Pecorino Romano*

¼ cup grated fontina

3 cloves fresh garlic – minced

3 ounces Italian sausage (or Homemade Sausage on page 142) – crumbled and cooked

½ small red pepper – seeded and diced

½ small shallot – minced

1 Tablespoon extra virgin olive oil

3 Tablespoons Fresh Pesto (page 55)

1 handful fresh arugula (optional)

- Preheat oven to 500° F. If you have a pizza stone, make sure that it is well preheated in the oven as well. Sprinkle cornmeal on pizza peel if using a pizza stone, or if you don't have a pizza stone, sprinkle cornmeal on a round baking sheet. Set aside.

- Roll out one ball of Pizza Dough, place on pizza peel if using a pizza stone, or on the prepared round baking sheet if you're not. Spread ricotta evenly over surface of dough.

- Top with remaining cheeses, garlic, and cooked Italian sausage.

- Using pizza peel, transfer pizza onto pizza stone, or simply place baking sheet with pizza into oven.

- Rotating the pizza a few times during baking to ensure even browning, bake pizza until crust is crisp and well-browned on all sides, about 8 to 10 minutes.

- While pizza is cooking, mix red pepper, shallots, and olive oil together in a small bowl.

- Remove pizza from oven, top with red pepper mixture, Fresh Pesto, and arugula.

- Slice and serve immediately.

Pear and Gorgonzola Pizza with Herbed Candied Walnuts

This pizza has a great contrast of flavors and is especially flavorful in autumn when pears are at their peak.

Serves 2-3

1 Tbsp fine ground cornmeal

1 ball Pizza Dough (page 43)

2 ounces Gorgonzola – crumbled

¾ cup shredded mozzarella

½ Bartlett pear – cored and sliced into thin wedges (if you want to use the whole pear, make two pizzas…)

3 Tablespoons Herbed Candied Walnuts (page 184)

¼ teaspoon kosher salt or to taste

- Preheat oven to 500° F. If you have a pizza stone, make sure that it is well preheated in the oven as well. Sprinkle cornmeal on pizza peel if using a pizza stone, or if you don't have a pizza stone, sprinkle cornmeal on a round baking sheet. Set aside.

- Roll out one ball of Pizza Dough, place on pizza peel if using a pizza stone, or on the prepared round baking sheet if you're not. Top dough with Gorgonzola, mozzarella, and pears.

- Using pizza peel, transfer pizza onto pizza stone, or simply place baking sheet with pizza into oven.

- Rotating the pizza a few times during baking to ensure even browning, bake pizza until crust is crisp and well-browned on all sides, about 8 minutes.

- Remove pizza from oven, top with Herbed Candied Walnuts, and sprinkle on salt.

- Slice and serve immediately.

Pasta

This chapter is the one, with the possible exception of the chapter on pizza, which gives people the most pause when contemplating tomato-free Italian cooking. But since pasta arrived in Italy before tomatoes, it can't be too much of a stretch to comprehend how this is possible.

As with all things Italian, the trick lies in the perfect cooking of the base ingredient – in this case the pasta – and then accompanying it with fabulous sauces and flavor combinations. In the case of pasta, the proper cooking technique is widely known as *al dente*, but it's very hard to describe in words what that feels like. If you've never felt *al dente* pasta, the best way to know if you have it right is to bite into a piece of pasta with your front teeth and feel the resistance it offers. If there is anything akin to a snap, crunch, or chew that you have to tear off with your teeth, you're not done yet. Keep cooking until there is a little bit of resistance, but nothing remotely unpleasant about it. If the pasta yields no resistance at all, and your teeth sink right through, you've overcooked your pasta, and you'll just have to start over. Perfect *al dente* texture lies between these two extremes and is wonderfully soft with a hint of firmness that makes it the perfect background for all pasta sauces.

The other thing to consider with pasta is the seemingly innumerable shapes. Generally, I consider pastas to come in two types of cuts: the "long cuts" like spaghetti, linguine and fettuccine, and the "short cuts" like penne, shells and ziti. Typically a given pasta sauce will be better suited for a long cut or a short cut pasta, and those are the ones I will recommend in my recipes. So while I have my own preferences and recommendations for which specific cut of pasta you should use with each sauce, please remember that the selection of pasta shape is ultimately subjective, and you should use whatever cut you most prefer. Remember, you're the chef – cook what you like!

FRESH PASTA

This simple recipe for pasta can be expanded easily using the ratio of 1 egg for ½ cup of flour. For 4 people, you will probably want to make about 3 or 4 eggs worth of fresh pasta, which will result in a little more than the equivalent of 1 pound of dried pasta, but works with sauce recipes that say they are for 1 pound of pasta.

1½ cups (7½ ounces) all-purpose flour

3 large eggs – room temperature is better, fresh is essential

1 Tablespoon extra virgin olive oil

¾ teaspoon kosher salt

- Mound flour in a large bowl, and make a well in the center.
- Crack eggs into the well; add olive oil and salt. With a fork, beat eggs, oil, and salt together in the well until the egg is well beaten. Continue to stir, slowly incorporating flour from the edges of the well into the egg mixture, turning the bowl to make sure the flour is added from all directions, and the well does not break.
- When you can no longer mix in more flour, and the dough is in a ball in the bowl, turn everything out onto a lightly floured surface. Knead until all of the flour from the bowl has been incorporated and mixture is smooth – if the dough is still sticky, work in some more flour.
- Divide the dough into 4 pieces. While working with one piece, keep the other pieces under a slightly damp towel.
- Run one piece of dough through the pasta machine at widest setting, fold dough twice into a third of its length, turn it one-quarter turn, and run through the machine again. Repeat until the dough is smooth and elastic, but not tough – about 8 to 12 passes through the machine total.
- After the last pass through the machine on the widest setting, fold the long edges of the dough in towards the center so they are just touching in the middle; this is the LAST fold for the dough. Tighten the rollers by one notch. Run the pasta through this setting once. Tighten the rollers one notch and run it through again.
- Repeat until the dough has reached the 7 to 9* setting, depending on how thick you want the pasta.
- Cut the pasta into your desired shape, or stuff it with filling if you're making a filled pasta at this point before working with the next piece of dough.
- Repeat these steps for rolling out and shaping the pasta with each of the other three pieces of dough.

- When the pasta is in the form you desire, cook by submerging in abundant salted boiling water for about 1 to 2 minutes until *al dente*.

- The pasta is now ready for your favorite sauce – just be sure not to rinse it off, or else the sauce won't stick to it.

*This assumes your machine has 9 settings – some only have 6 or 7. What you are looking for is pasta that is near or at the thinnest setting – but ultimately the final decision on how thin to make the pasta is your personal preference!

FRESH PESTO

This pesto is good for any and all recipes that call for pesto. It's not only great on pasta, but it can also be mixed with ricotta or mascarpone for crostini, and can even be stirred into soups. Pesto can be frozen before you add the cheese. Just thaw and add cheese – it's a great way to surprise your guests with a fresh basil pesto in the middle of winter.

Makes about 1 cup

2 cups fresh basil leaves – rinsed and patted dry

3 Tablespoons pine nuts – lightly toasted

2 cloves garlic – coarsely chopped

½ cup extra virgin olive oil

½ cup freshly grated *Parmigiano Reggiano*

Kosher salt

Freshly ground black pepper

- Place basil, pine nuts, and garlic in a food processor or blender and pulse until finely chopped. You may have to stop and scrape down the sides once or twice.
- Turn blender on, and leave blades spinning while you slowly add olive oil.
- When all of the olive oil has been incorporated, and the mixture is emulsified; transfer to a medium bowl, and stir in Parmesan by hand.
- Season to taste with salt and pepper.

PISTACHIO PESTO

I've tried many recipes for pistachio pesto, which I first tried in a beachfront trattoria in Sicily. The color was light green and the flavors made me fall to my knees. It took me lots of practice and samples to find what I was looking for, but I think this is the best I can do without having to track that trattoria down. But then again, that might be fun too!

Serves 4-6

2 dried black mission figs – stems removed

¼ cup hot water

¾ cup pistachios – shelled and lightly toasted

¼ cup fresh basil leaves

¼ cup fresh flat leaf parsley leaves

Kosher salt

½ cup extra virgin olive oil

¼ cup freshly grated *Parmigiano Reggiano*

Freshly ground black pepper

1 pound dried pasta – a short cut like rotini is perfect for this sauce

Garnish:

2 Tablespoons roughly chopped pistachios – toasted

1 Tablespoon thinly sliced fresh basil

1 Tablespoon roughly chopped fresh flat leaf parsley

2 Tablespoons freshly grated *Parmigiano Reggiano*

Freshly ground black pepper

- In a small bowl, combine figs and hot water, and set aside until figs are softened, about 20 minutes. Reserve figs and water separately.
- Bring a large pot of salted water to a boil over high heat.
- In a blender or food processor, pulse pistachios, basil, parsley, and ½ teaspoon salt a few times to chop them thoroughly. Scrape down the sides of the bowl.
- Add rehydrated figs to the pistachio mixture, and pulse a few times.
- In a separate small bowl, whisk together olive oil and reserved fig water. With the blades running in the food processor, slowly add the oil mixture to the pistachios in the food processor. Puree mixture until mostly smooth.
- Transfer mixture from the blender to a small bowl, and fold in Parmesan. Season to taste with salt and pepper. Set aside.

- Add pasta to boiling water and cook until *al dente*. Reserve ¼ cup of the cooking liquid, and drain the pasta. Mix pasta with pesto, and add the cooking liquid by tablespoons as needed to thin the pesto so it will evenly coat the pasta.
- Serve pasta garnished with pistachios, basil, parsley, Parmesan, and pepper.

Arugula Pesto

This is a great variation on pesto, though the concept is still the same. There's no change to the technique, and the ingredients are very similar. This is a much more peppery sauce, so the uses for this sauce are not as varied as traditional pesto, but this is an especially great sauce for coating a bed of the Herb and Cheese Ravioli (page 72). If the arugula is particularly peppery, you may want to omit the black pepper and/or the cayenne.

Makes about 1 cup

2 cups packed fresh arugula leaves – preferably wild

3 Tablespoons walnuts – lightly toasted

2 cloves garlic – chopped coarsely

½ cup extra virgin olive oil

¼ cup freshly grated *Parmigiano Reggiano*

¼ cup freshly grated *Pecorino Romano*

Pinch cayenne pepper (optional)

Kosher salt

Freshly ground black pepper

- Rinse arugula and pat it dry.
- Place arugula, walnuts, and garlic in a food processor or blender and pulse until finely chopped. You may have to stop and scrape down the sides once or twice.
- Turn blender on, and leave blades spinning while you slowly add olive oil.
- When all of the olive oil has been incorporated, and the mixture is emulsified; transfer to a medium bowl, and stir in Parmesan and *Pecorino Romano* by hand.
- Taste pesto first, then adjust seasonings with cayenne, salt, and black pepper.

Fettuccine Alfredo

A cookbook covering the great foods of Italy that have no tomatoes would be remiss if it excluded this fabulous and famous sauce from its ranks. It is, of course, classically served on fettuccine – serving it on homemade fettuccine is one of the great treats you can give yourself. And of course, be sure to use only high quality *Parmigiano Reggiano* and Gorgonzola.

Serves 4-6

½ cup dry white wine

1½ cups heavy cream

½ cup (1 stick) butter

3 eggs of Fresh Pasta (page 53) – fettuccine cut is most traditional (or 1 pound dried fettuccine)

2 ounces freshly grated *Parmigiano Reggiano* – plus more for garnish

2 ounces Gorgonzola Dolce

Kosher salt

Freshly ground black pepper

Freshly grated nutmeg

- Bring a large pot of salted water to a boil over high heat.
- In a large skillet over medium-high heat, cook wine down until 2 Tablespoons remain.
- Add cream and butter, and reduce heat to medium. Reduce sauce slightly at a light simmer, stirring to prevent burning.
- Add pasta to the boiling water and cook until *al dente*.
- Drain pasta and add to sauce in skillet. Stir in Parmesan and Gorgonzola. Cook at a light simmer for about 1 minute.
- Season to taste with salt, pepper, and nutmeg.
- Serve immediately, preferably on warmed plates so as to keep the sauce smooth. Pass extra Parmesan at the table.

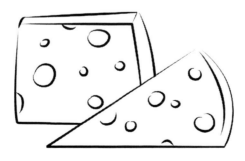

SPAGHETTI ALLA CARBONARA

Another classic Roman pasta sauce, Spaghetti alla Carbonara is one of the most soul-satisfying comfort foods I know. Alas, it is not the most healthful dish ever created, so it should be enjoyed by people who are not currently dieting, and even then only in moderation. But still, I can't think of a better dish to warm me all the way through on a cold winter night.

Serves 4-6

½ pound bacon, pancetta, or *guanciale* – cut into small pieces (about ½-inch)

2 cloves garlic – minced

¼ cup dry white wine

½ teaspoon crushed red pepper

½ cup heavy cream

3 Tablespoons butter – softened

3 large eggs

¾ cup freshly grated *Parmigiano Reggiano* – plus extra for garnish

¼ cup freshly grated *Pecorino Romano*

3 eggs of Fresh Pasta (page 53) – spaghetti cut is most traditional (or 1 pound dried spaghetti)

Kosher salt

Freshly ground black pepper

- Bring a large pot of salted water to a boil over high heat.
- In a medium skillet over medium heat, cook bacon until almost crispy. Pour off about one-half of the fat, keeping about 3 to 4 Tablespoons of fat (and the bacon) in the pan.
- Add garlic, cook until fragrant, about 1 minute.
- Add white wine and deglaze the pan by cooking, stirring to scrape up all of the browned bits on the bottom of the pan, until almost all the wine is gone.
- Add crushed red pepper and cream to the hot pan, and bring to a simmer. As soon as cream is simmering, turn off heat, and leave pan on warm burner. Stir occasionally while completing the recipe.
- In separate bowl, cream butter with wooden spoon until soft and fluffy. Add eggs, and stir to combine. Add cheeses and stir to combine. Set aside.
- Add pasta to the boiling water and cook until *al dente*.
- When pasta is done, drain and transfer to a large serving bowl.
- Add cream mixture to the pasta, and toss to combine.
- Add cheese mixture to the pasta, and toss again to combine.
- Season to taste with salt and pepper and serve immediately with extra Parmesan and freshly ground black pepper at the table.

LINGUINE WITH LEMON, CREAM, AND RAPINI

The combination of flavors, textures, and colors in this dish made it seem like a great idea when I first wrote it down. But it was only when I finally made it for a class I was teaching that I realized there was really something special going on here.

Serves 4-6

1 pound rapini (broccoli rabe) – rinsed, dried, trimmed, and coarsely chopped

¼ pound pancetta or bacon – chopped

Kosher salt

Freshly ground black pepper

3 eggs of Fresh Pasta (page 53) – cut into linguine (or 1 pound dried linguine)

4 large egg yolks

Zest of 2 lemons – divided

½ cup + 2 Tablespoons freshly grated *Parmigiano Reggiano* – plus extra for garnish

½ cup + 2 Tablespoons heavy cream – at room temperature

6 Tablespoons milk – at room temperature

3 Tablespoons chopped fresh flat leaf parsley

2 Tablespoons chopped fresh chives

- Bring a large pot of salted water to a boil over high heat.
- Add rapini and cook until stems are tender, about 3 to 5 minutes. Drain rapini, reserving cooking water. Rinse rapini gently under cold water to stop cooking. Squeeze any excess water out of rapini, and set aside.
- In a large skillet over medium-high heat, cook pancetta until almost crispy, about 4 minutes. Add rapini and cook for about 3 minutes more. Season to taste with salt and pepper, and set aside in a large serving bowl.
- Bring the rapini cooking water back to a boil. Add linguine and cook until *al dente*. Drain and place in the large serving bowl with the rapini.
- While pasta is cooking, whisk together egg yolks, zest of one lemon, Parmesan, and a few grinds of black pepper in a small bowl. Then whisk in cream, milk, parsley, and chives.
- Combine the cream mixture with the rapini and pasta in the bowl. Stir to combine.
- Serve immediately garnished with remaining lemon zest and some extra Parmesan.

ORECCHIETTE WITH PORCINI MUSHROOM AND CREAM SAUCE

Going a little north of Rome into Umbria, we find this fabulous cream sauce that beautifully hums with porcini mushrooms. In Italy, fresh porcinis are what are used; but for some reason, porcinis are usually available only dried in the United States. If you can find fresh, use them!

Serves 4-6

1½ ounces dried porcini mushrooms (or 1 pound fresh)

2 cups hot water

3 Tablespoons olive oil

2 small shallots – thinly sliced

3 cloves garlic – minced

½ cup dry white wine

¼ teaspoon crushed red pepper

3 eggs of Fresh Pasta (page 53) – shaped into orecchiette (or 1 pound of dried orecchiette)

1 cup heavy cream

2 Tablespoons fresh lemon juice

3 Tablespoons chopped fresh parsley

Kosher salt

Freshly ground black pepper

Fresh fennel fronds – for garnish

Lemon zest – for garnish

- Soak dried porcinis in hot water for 20 minutes to rehydrate. Reserve ¼ cup of the soaking water. Drain and chop porcinis. Set aside. (If using fresh porcinis, slice them and set them aside.)

- Bring a large pot of salted water to a boil over high heat.

- In a large skillet over medium heat, add olive oil, and then shallots. Cook gently until shallots are translucent.

- Add garlic, and cook until fragrant, about 30 seconds.

- Add mushrooms and sauté for 3 minutes. (You may need to sauté for 5 minutes if you're using fresh porcinis.)

- Add wine, reserved ¼ cup mushroom soaking liquid, and red pepper. Bring sauce to a light simmer.

- While sauce is simmering, add orecchiette to the boiling water and cook until *al dente*.

- As pasta is finishing cooking, add cream, lemon juice, and parsley to the mushroom sauce, and bring to a simmer again.

- When pasta is done, drain and pour into a large serving bowl.
- Season the mushroom sauce to taste with salt and pepper, and pour over pasta. Toss to coat, and then serve, garnished with fresh fennel fronds and lemon zest.

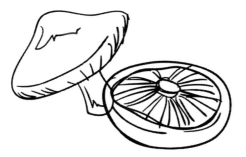

Farfalle with Mascarpone, Asparagus, Hazelnuts, and Smoked Salt

A friend of mine gave me the idea for this dish. I liked it, as it uses asparagus, nuts, and mascarpone – all typical Northern Italian ingredients. If you can't find smoked salt, which adds a wonderful extra flavor to this dish, coarse sea salt works very well.

Serves 4-6

1 pound slender asparagus

3 Tablespoons extra virgin olive oil

Kosher salt

Freshly ground black pepper

3 eggs of Fresh Pasta (page 53) – cut into farfalle (or 1 pound dried farfalle)

1 (8-ounce) container mascarpone

$\frac{1}{3}$ cup Gorgonzola

$\frac{1}{2}$ cup hazelnuts, husked, toasted, coarsely chopped

3 Tablespoons chopped fresh chives

Smoked salt (or coarse sea salt) – for garnish

- Preheat broiler in oven.
- Snap off the tough ends from asparagus spears. If spears are any thicker than pencils, lightly peel the stalks to remove the tough skin.
- In a bowl, toss asparagus with olive oil and season lightly with salt and pepper.
- Broil asparagus spears until browned on both sides, about 2 to 3 minutes each side. Remove asparagus from oven and cut into 1-inch lengths. Set aside.
- Bring a large pot of salted water to a boil over high heat.
- Add pasta to the boiling water and cook until *al dente*. Reserve 1 cup of the pasta cooking water. Drain pasta and return it to the pot it cooked in.
- Stir in mascarpone, Gorgonzola, and asparagus. Over medium-low heat, toss together until pasta is coated with sauce and mixture is heated through, about 4 minutes. If pasta seems dry, add a little of the reserved cooking water as needed to moisten.
- Remove pasta from heat, add hazelnuts and chives.
- Serve onto plates, garnishing each serving with smoked salt.

Pasta

FETTUCCINE WITH BRUSSELS SPROUTS, PINE NUTS, AND BUTTER

Brussels sprouts are one of those vegetables that I thought were terrible when I was a kid, only because I never knew how to cook them properly. Luckily, I had a Brussels sprouts revolution, and they are now one of my favorite vegetables to work with. This is just one of many great Brussels sprouts dishes I have created through my experimentation in the kitchen.

Serves 4-6

8 Tablespoons unsalted butter – divided

1 white onion – diced

2 cloves garlic – minced

1¼ pounds fresh Brussels sprouts – cleaned, thinly shaved

2 Tablespoons dry white wine

3 eggs of Fresh Pasta (page 53) – fettuccine cut (or 1 pound dried fettuccine)

5 Tablespoons pine nuts – toasted

2 Tablespoons fresh lemon juice

¼ cup chopped fresh flat leaf parsley

½ teaspoon freshly grated nutmeg

2 Tablespoons extra virgin olive oil

Kosher salt

Freshly ground black pepper

Freshly grated *Parmigiano Reggiano* – for garnish

- Bring a large pot of salted water to a boil over high heat.
- Melt 3 Tablespoons butter in a large skillet over medium-high heat. Sauté onions until lightly colored.
- Add garlic, cook until fragrant, about 30 seconds.
- Add Brussels sprouts, cook until lightly browned. Add wine and deglaze the pan by cooking, stirring to scrape up all of the browned bits on the bottom of the pan, until almost all the wine is gone.
- Add pasta to the boiling water and cook until *al dente*.
- When pasta is done, drain, and return it to the pot it cooked in.
- Add shaved Brussels sprouts and remaining 5 Tablespoons butter to the cooked pasta in the pot. Toss to combine.
- Add pine nuts, lemon juice, parsley, nutmeg, and olive oil. Season to taste with salt and pepper.
- Serve immediately, and pass grated Parmesan at table.

SMOKED SALMON FETTUCCINE WITH LEMON BUTTER SAUCE

This inspiration for this dish came to me when I tasted a batch of my father's incredible hot-smoked salmon. I loved the rich smoky flavor so much and knew it would be enhanced with a creamy sauce since smoke and cream blend so well. The addition of lemon was my mom's idea, so this truly is a "family" sauce. Be sure to use hot-smoked salmon, which is dry, instead of cold-smoked salmon, like lox, which is too moist.

Serves 4-6

1 leek

3 eggs of Fresh Pasta (page 53) – fettuccine cut (or 1 pound dried fettuccine)

1 Tablespoon olive oil

2 cloves garlic   minced

3 Tablespoons dry white wine

¼ cup fresh lemon juice

1 Tablespoon capers – drained and rinsed

5 Tablespoons cold butter – cut into tablespoons

3 Tablespoons heavy cream

Kosher salt

White pepper

4-5 ounces hot-smoked salmon – flaked into 1-inch pieces

3 Tablespoons chopped fresh flat leaf parsley – divided

- Bring a large pot of salted water to a boil over high heat.
- Cut off and discard dark green parts and root end of leek. Slice leek in half lengthwise, and wash out any dirt between the layers.
- Slice white and light green parts of leek into thin semi-circle slices. Set aside the white and light green parts of the leek separately.
- If using dried pasta, drop the fettuccine into the boiling water and cook until *al dente*. While pasta cooks, put sauce together. (If using fresh pasta, you can cook it right near the end, since it cooks so quickly.)
- Heat olive oil in a large skillet over medium-high heat; add garlic and white part of the leek. Sauté until leek is translucent.
- Add white wine and deglaze pan by cooking, stirring to scrape up all of the browned bits on the bottom of the pan, until almost all the wine is gone. Add lemon juice and reduce by half. You should have about 2 Tablespoons liquid in pan.
- Add capers to lemon juice mixture and remove pan from heat.

- With the pan still off the heat, melt in butter, 1 Tablespoon at a time.
- Add cream and stir to combine. Season to taste with salt and white pepper.
- When pasta is done, drain, and add to skillet with sauce. Toss to coat pasta completely.
- Add smoked salmon, reserved light green part of the leek, and 2 Tablespoons parsley.
- Serve pasta onto plates and garnish with remaining parsley. Serve immediately.

Penne with Roasted Red Peppers, Sausage, and Ricotta

This dish really highlights the flavors of Roasted Red Peppers (page 179) in a combination that just can't be beat. The sausages can be hot or sweet, depending on your preference. If you want a slightly more healthful version, you can always use slices of grilled chicken breast.

Serves 4-6

6 ounces (¾ cup) fresh whole milk ricotta

1 Tablespoon vegetable oil

¾ pound Italian sausage (or Homemade Sausage – page 142) – removed from casings and crumbled

1 onion – halved and thinly sliced

3 Roasted Red Peppers (page 179)

2 cloves garlic

1½ Tablespoons chopped fresh flat leaf parsley

3 Tablespoons chopped fresh basil

¼ teaspoon crushed red pepper

3 Tablespoons extra virgin olive oil

Kosher salt

Freshly ground black pepper

1 pound penne pasta

½ cup freshly grated *Parmigiano Reggiano*

10 fresh sage leaves – thinly sliced

1 Tablespoon capers – drained and rinsed (optional)

- Bring a large pot of salted water to a boil over high heat.
- If ricotta is especially wet, spread the ricotta on a double layer of paper towels. Lay another 2 paper towels on top, and press down to remove excess moisture from the cheese. Set aside.
- Preheat oven to 200° F. Line a plate with paper towels.
- Heat a large skillet over medium heat. Add vegetable oil and then sausage. Cook sausage until cooked through, about 4 minutes. Using a slotted spoon, remove sausage to the lined plate, leaving fat behind in the pan. Place the plate in the warm oven.
- Discard all but 2 Tablespoons fat from the pan. Increase heat to medium-high.
- Add onions to the pan and cook quickly until softened. Transfer onions to the plate with sausages, and keep warm in the oven.
- Place roasted peppers, garlic, parsley, basil, and red pepper in a food processor. Pulse a few times, and then, with the blades running, slowly add olive oil. Transfer from the food processor to a small bowl. Season to taste with salt and pepper.

- Add penne to the boiling water and cook until *al dente*. Reserve ½ cup of the cooking water.
- When the pasta is done, drain and return to the pot it cooked in. Stir in the red pepper puree, sausage mixture, and Parmesan. If pasta is dry, stir in some cooking water to make it the right consistency.
- Place in serving bowl or on individual plates and garnish with the ricotta, sage, and capers. Serve immediately.

Pumpkin Raviolini with Salvia

The flavors of pumpkin and sage (*salvia*) with a hint of almonds make this a truly delicious Northern Italian flavor combination. These raviolini can be remarkably filling though, so if you're serving them as a first course, be sure not to make too many or your guests won't have room for your main course. Amaretti biscuits are wonderful dry Italian cookies with an intense almond flavor. Use ground almonds as a replacement if you can't find them.

Serves 4-6

1 (15-ounce) can pureed pumpkin (not pumpkin pie filling)

2 small Amaretti biscuits – finely crumbled (or 2 Tablespoons ground toasted almonds plus 1 pinch sugar)

1¼ cups freshly grated *Parmigiano Reggiano* – divided

Kosher salt

Freshly ground black pepper

3 eggs of Fresh Pasta (page 53) – left as sheets

Cornmeal for dusting

6 Tablespoons butter

4-5 sprigs fresh sage – plus extra leaves for garnish

- Spread three layers of paper towels on a baking sheet and spread pumpkin onto the paper towels in a wide, thin sheet. Place three more layers of paper towels on top of pumpkin and press down. After 10 minutes, replace top towels with 3 fresh layers; press down again and wait 10 to 20 more minutes to absorb as much moisture as possible from the pumpkin. Using a rubber spatula, scrape the pumpkin into a medium bowl.

- Combine pumpkin with crumbled Amaretti and ¾ cup Parmesan. Season to taste with salt and pepper.

- Make the fresh pasta, rolling out each sheet and making the raviolini with that sheet before working on the next sheet of pasta.

- To assemble raviolini: When the sheet of pasta has reached desired thickness (about setting 8 on the pasta machine), cut in half. Place small dollops of pumpkin filling (about the size of a gumball) on one of the two sheets, spaced out about every 2 to 3 inches.

- Brush the other sheet lightly with water. Place the moistened sheet over the top of the sheet with the filling (moist side down), and use a small cookie or biscuit cutter to cut out the raviolini. Use a fork to seal up the edges.

- Set aside finished raviolini to dry on a baking sheet dusted with cornmeal while making the rest of the raviolini.

- Melt butter in a small saucepan or skillet over medium heat. Add sage sprigs and cook until sage is wilted, and butter is lightly browned and is no longer frothing. Discard sage, and keep this *salvia* sauce warm while pasta is cooking.

- Over high heat, bring a large pot of salted water to a light boil. Carefully drop in about 12 to 15 of the raviolini and cook at a gentle boil until the pasta is *al dente,* about 2 to 3 minutes. Using a slotted spoon, carefully remove the raviolini from the water, and place them in a colander to drain completely.

- Place a few raviolini on a pasta serving plate and drizzle *salvia* sauce over the raviolini. Garnish plates using remaining Parmesan, and a few fresh sage leaves. Serve immediately.

Herb and Cheese Ravioli with Fresh Carrot Sauce

The fresh herbs in these ravioli make the cheese-based filling seem light and fresh. Paired with this creamy Fresh Carrot Sauce, it's a feast for the eyes as well as the taste buds. Be sure not to just slop on the sauce. You put in the work to make the beautiful ravioli, so make sure your guests see them! These ravioli are also excellent with the Arugula Pesto (page 58) and the Carrot Sauce is perfect on the Spinach and Ricotta Gnocchi (page 81).

Serves 4-6

Ravioli:

4 ounces whole milk ricotta

4 ounces goat cheese

$^{1}/_{3}$ cup freshly grated *Parmigiano Reggiano*   plus extra for garnish

¼ cup mascarpone cheese

1 Tablespoon chopped fresh basil

2 teaspoons chopped fresh mint

1 teaspoon chopped fresh oregano

¼ teaspoon ground nutmeg

Kosher salt

Freshly ground black pepper

3 eggs of Fresh Pasta (page 53) – left as sheets

Cornmeal – for dusting

Fresh Carrot Sauce:

2 cups water

Kosher salt

3 large carrots (about 8 ounces) – peeled and sliced in 1-inch pieces

2 cloves garlic

1 Tablespoon chopped fresh fennel fronds – plus extra for garnish

1 teaspoon chopped fresh flat leaf parsley

¼ cup fresh orange juice

¼ cup heavy cream

Freshly ground black pepper

Extra virgin olive oil for drizzling

-   If ricotta is especially wet, spread the ricotta on a double layer of paper towels. Lay another 2 paper towels on top, and press down to remove excess moisture from the cheese.

- In a bowl, mix ricotta, goat cheese, Parmesan, mascarpone, herbs, and nutmeg together. Season to taste with salt and pepper.
- Roll out pasta sheets, place small dollops (about the size of a gumball) of filling along the bottom half of the sheet, spaced out about every 2 to 3 inches.
- Brush the top half of pasta sheet with water, then fold it in half over the filling.
- Using a knife, pizza cutter, or pasta wheel, cut ravioli out from the sheet, and use the tines of a fork to seal the edges.
- As you make the ravioli, place them on a large rimmed baking sheet dusted with cornmeal. Continue until all the ravioli are made, set them aside on the baking sheet while you make Fresh Carrot Sauce.
- Bring a large pot of salted water to a boil over high heat.
- Prepare Fresh Carrot Sauce: In a small saucepan, bring water with 2 teaspoons salt to a boil. Add carrots and garlic, and simmer until the carrots are tender, about 8 minutes. Reserve 1 cup cooking water. Drain thoroughly.
- Place carrots and garlic in a blender; add fennel, parsley, and orange juice. Puree until smooth. If the mixture is too dry, add some of the reserved carrot cooking water to the mixture – just enough to make sure it can puree smoothly – don't add so much as to make the sauce thin. The final sauce should be able to puree smoothly in the blender, but not be watery in consistency.
- Scrape out puree into a small saucepan and stir in heavy cream. Season to taste with salt and pepper, and keep warm in a saucepan over low heat while cooking the pasta.
- Add ravioli to the boiling water in batches and cook until ravioli float, and then cook for an additional 30 seconds.
- Using a slotted spoon, transfer ravioli to a large bowl. Toss lightly with extra virgin olive oil to keep them from sticking together. Repeat with more batches of ravioli until all are cooked, and all are coated lightly in oil.
- To serve, spread some of the Carrot Sauce on individual plates. Divide the cooked raviolis among the plates. Top the ravioli with just a little more of the Carrot Sauce. Garnish with fresh fennel fronds and a few gratings of Parmesan and serve immediately.

LINGUINE ALLE VONGOLE

Pasta with clam sauce comes in both red and white versions – considering the theme of this book, we will of course create the white version. This pasta comes together very quickly in the pan, so you must have all your ingredients ready to go before you begin cooking. If you're using dried pasta, you can put the sauce together while the pasta cooks. Fresh pasta cooks so fast, you can just cook it when the sauce is done. This pasta is so easy, you can even make it as a quick lunch!

Serves 2-3

25 littleneck clams

2 eggs of Fresh Pasta (page 53) – cut into linguine (or ½ pound dried linguine)

1 Tablespoon extra virgin olive oil

2 ounces pancetta (or bacon) – cut in thin strips

2 cloves garlic – chopped

2 Tablespoons roughly chopped fresh basil – plus extra for garnish

½ cup dry white wine or light beer

2 teaspoons capers – drained and rinsed

Kosher salt

Dash crushed red pepper – plus extra for garnish

- Bring a large pot of salted water to a boil over high heat.
- Before you do anything else, clean clams by scrubbing them under running cold water. Be sure they're able to close up completely to prove they are still alive. Throw out any that won't close.
- If using dried pasta, drop pasta into the boiling water. Stir, and have pasta cook while you put the sauce together. (If using fresh pasta, you can cook it when the sauce is done.)
- Heat olive oil in a large skillet over medium-high heat. Add pancetta, and cook until fat begins to render and pancetta is lightly cooked.
- Add garlic and sauté until garlic has a little bit of color, about one minute.
- Once garlic has some color, add clams, basil, wine, capers, salt to taste, and red pepper; shake the pan a few times to combine the ingredients. Cover the skillet and continue to cook until steam begins to escape from under the lid.
- Remove the cover and check to see if clams are all open at this point. If they aren't, return the cover for 30 more seconds. If they are done, remove the cover.
- Take clams out of the pan and place them in a large bowl. The easiest way to do this is with tongs. Lift clams by placing one of the tong ends inside clam and gripping one of the two shells. Then be sure to tip the clam to drain all the natural juice out of clam and into the sauce.

- When pasta is *al dente*, drain pasta and add it to the skillet with the sauce and toss a few times to combine and coat pasta thoroughly. Cook pasta together with the sauce for 1 minute.
- Serve pasta onto plates, and distribute clams evenly among plates. Garnish with extra basil and/or crushed red pepper.

Squid Ink Pasta with Tarragon Butter and Roasted Prosciutto

This pasta was created when I was asked to create a multiple-course Venetian meal for a wine-pairing dinner. I served it with seared scallops on top, which you can always do yourself, but the pasta by itself is magnificent.

Serves 4-6

7 Tablespoons butter – softened

1 bunch (about 3-4 Tablespoons) fresh tarragon – chopped, plus 1 Tablespoon for garnish

Kosher salt

1 pound squid ink pasta (long cut, like spaghetti or linguine)

½ recipe Oven-Roasted Prosciutto (page 183)

2 scallions – cut on the diagonal into ¼-inch slices

¼ cup Roasted Red Pepper (page 179) – chopped coarsely

Sea salt flakes – for garnish

- Bring a large pot of salted water to a boil over high heat.
- Mix butter and chopped tarragon together in a small bowl. Season to taste with salt and set aside.
- Add pasta to the boiling water and cook until *al dente*.
- While pasta is cooking, heat a large skillet over low heat. Add butter mixture and allow it to melt – don't let butter or tarragon brown.
- When pasta is done, drain and shake out all excess moisture. Add to tarragon butter in skillet and toss to coat.
- Add Oven Roasted Prosciutto, scallions, and Roasted Red Peppers; toss to combine.
- Divide pasta into portions and garnish with tarragon leaves and sea salt. Serve immediately.

LINGUINE WITH SPINACH AND OLIVES

This is a great recipe with so many natural flavors that all stand out yet work together at the same time. It's hard to think of a recipe that is easier to put together. Use high quality olives and cheese to make this recipe work perfectly. For more color, feel free to mix in some green olives with your black olives. If you have all your ingredients prepped, this sauce comes together very quickly, so if you're using dried pasta, don't even start cooking the sauce until the pasta is boiling away.

Serves 4-6

3 eggs of Fresh Pasta (page 53) – cut into linguine (or 1 pound dried linguine)

6 Tablespoons olive oil

2 cloves garlic – minced

1 Tablespoon capers – drained and rinsed

1 cup sliced black olives

8 ounces fresh baby spinach leaves – rinsed and dried

½-1 teaspoon crushed red pepper

3 ounces crumbled goat cheese

2 Tablespoons mascarpone cheese

¼ cup freshly grated *Parmigiano Reggiano* – plus extra for garnish

- Bring a large pot of salted water to a boil over high heat. Add linguine and begin cooking.
- In a large skillet, over medium-high heat, heat olive oil. Add garlic, capers, and olives. It may splatter some, so be careful and have a screen on hand.
- When olives are heated through, about 1 minute, add spinach and red pepper to the pan. Cook spinach, stirring regularly, until spinach has released most of its water. Keep mixture warm over low heat until pasta is done.
- When pasta is *al dente*, reserve 1 cup of the pasta cooking water and drain pasta.
- Add cooked pasta to the skillet with spinach and olives. Toss to combine thoroughly over low heat.
- In a small bowl, mix together goat cheese, mascarpone, and Parmesan. Stir the cheeses into pasta, allowing them to melt together over low heat. If pasta seems dry, add cooking water as needed to keep the mixture moist.
- Serve immediately, with additional Parmesan at the table.

POTATO GNOCCHI

A great batch of gnocchi is a sublimely filling treat. Potatoes are made into a pasta that feels lighter than air in your mouth, yet is rich and satisfying. Almost every Italian cookbook in the world has a different method of making gnocchi, and I've tried every one I've come across. I find this method of steaming the potatoes to be both the fastest method and the one that produces the best results.

Serves 4-8

¾ pound Russet potatoes (about 1 large) – cleaned, left whole, skin on

¾ pound Yukon gold potatoes (about 2 medium) – cleaned, left whole, skin on

1¼ cups all-purpose flour

1 teaspoon kosher salt

¼ teaspoon freshly ground black pepper

- Place potatoes in a steamer and steam them until fully cooked and tender, about 30 to 45 minutes. Remove from steamer; set aside until cool enough to handle.

- Bring a small pot of lightly salted water to a boil over high heat.

- Remove skins from potatoes, and pass potatoes through a food mill or a ricer into a large bowl to make them as smooth as possible.

- Using a fork, mix potatoes, flour, salt, and pepper together as much as possible, then turn out onto a clean, lightly floured work surface. Knead dough until it comes together and is smooth, about 1 to 2 minutes.

- Separate dough into 4 equal pieces. Roll one of the pieces out into a "snake" about ¾-inch to 1-inch thick. Cut off just three or four ¾-inch pieces from the snake. Roll them lightly against the tines of a fork with your thumb, pressing ridges into the gnocchi while making a dent in the side with your thumb.

- Drop these test gnocchi in the small pot of lightly boiling water. When they rise to the surface, count to 10, then transfer them to a plate with a slotted spoon. If they are falling apart in the water, the dough needs more flour. If they held together, taste them and see if the seasoning is correct in the dough. If they are undercooked, make a note and add a few seconds to the cooking time.

- Once the gnocchi are good to go, continue to roll out the rest of the dough and form them into individual gnocchi. If you are going to cook them later that day, spread finished gnocchi on a floured baking sheet and place in fridge.

- When all gnocchi are shaped, cook gnocchi in batches of 20 to 30 at a time in a large pot of salted boiling water until all gnocchi are cooked. Mix with sauce and serve immediately.

Sauces: While gnocchi admittedly go great with tomato cream sauces, there are several other sauces that work well with these dumplings. Pesto and gnocchi are a match made in heaven. If you are looking for an especially filling meal, gnocchi carbonara is incredibly decadent. Lastly a sauce of Gorgonzola and cream is also a real showstopper.

WILD MUSHROOM GNOCCHI

The addition of dried mushroom powder and a beaten egg make these gnocchi a different variation of the traditional potato gnocchi. Gnocchi made with eggs are in the "*Parigina*" (Parisian) style. They have a totally different texture, so it's up to you to try them both and decide which way you prefer! Who knew Italian cooking would be so challenging?

Serves 4-8

¾ pound Russet potatoes (about 1 large) – scrubbed, left whole, skin on

¾ pound Yukon gold potatoes (about 2 medium) – scrubbed, left whole, skin on

1 ounce dried wild mushrooms (porcini, or a mix)

1 large egg – lightly beaten

1-1¼ cups all-purpose flour

1 teaspoon kosher salt

¼ teaspoon freshly ground black pepper

- Place potatoes in a steamer over simmering water and steam them until fully cooked, about 45 minutes. Remove from steamer and set aside until cool enough to handle.

- Bring a small pot of lightly salted water to a boil over high heat.

- Remove skins from potatoes, and pass potatoes through a food mill or a ricer into a large bowl to make them as smooth as possible.

- Place mushrooms in a food processor and pulse several times to make a fine powder.

- Add mushroom powder, egg, flour, salt, and pepper to potatoes. Mix together with fork as much as possible, then turn out onto a clean, lightly floured work surface. Knead dough until it comes together and is smooth, about 1 to 2 minutes.

- Separate dough into 4 equal pieces. Roll one of the pieces out into a "snake" about ¾-inch to 1-inch thick. Cut off three or four ¾-inch pieces. Roll them lightly against the tines of a fork with your thumb, pressing ridges into the back side of the gnocchi while making a dent in the side with your thumb.

- Drop these test gnocchi in the pot of lightly boiling water. When they rise to the surface, count to 10, then remove them with a slotted spoon. If they are falling apart in the water, the dough needs more flour. If they held together, taste them and see if the seasoning is correct in the dough. If they are undercooked, make a note and add a few seconds to the cooking time.

- Once the gnocchi are good to go, continue to roll out the rest of the dough and form them into individual gnocchi. Spread finished gnocchi on a floured baking sheet and place in fridge if you are going to cook them later.

- When all gnocchi are shaped, cook gnocchi in batches of 20 to 30 at a time in a large pot of salted boiling water until all gnocchi are cooked. Mix with sauce and serve immediately.

Sauces: The Salvia Sauce from the Pumpkin Raviolini with Salvia (page 70) is an incredible accompaniment to these gnocchi.

SPINACH-RICOTTA GNOCCHI

These gnocchi aren't based on a potato recipe, they are more in the *gnudi* style, which is to say, they are in essence a ravioli filling that is then cooked without the pasta around them. This gnudi style is a little more challenging to work with, but the results will still be very light and sure to please everyone.

Serves 4-8

1 Tablespoon olive oil

2¼ pounds (36 ounces) fresh baby spinach

½ small onion – minced

2 cloves garlic – minced

1½ cups fresh whole milk ricotta

1¼ cups all-purpose flour – plus extra for dusting

¾ cup freshly grated *Parmigiano Reggiano*

2 large egg yolks – lightly beaten

¼ teaspoon freshly grated nutmeg

1 teaspoon kosher salt

¼ teaspoon freshly ground black pepper

- In a large skillet over medium-high heat, warm olive oil. Add spinach, onion, and garlic, and sauté while constantly stirring, until the spinach has released most of its water, about 3 to 4 minutes. Do in two batches if necessary.

- Transfer the spinach mixture to a strainer, and press out all the excess water. Place on a cutting board and finely chop. Place spinach in a large bowl and allow to cool until it is room temperature, or just slightly warm.

- Mix in ricotta, flour, Parmesan, and egg yolks. Stir completely, but don't over-mix. Add nutmeg, salt, and pepper. Taste and adjust seasoning.

- Bring a small pot of lightly salted water to a boil over high heat.

- Place a small amount of flour (about ½ cup) in a small bowl. Flour your hands with some extra flour. Form one or two balls of the gnocchi mixture with your hands (you will not be able to shape these like the traditional potato gnocchi – just make balls about ¾- to 1-inch in diameter) and roll them in the extra flour.

- Drop these test gnocchi into the boiling water and when they rise to the surface, count to 10, then remove with a slotted spoon. If they are falling apart in the water, the dough needs more flour. If they held together, taste them and see if the seasoning is correct in the dough. If they are undercooked, make a note and add a few seconds to the cooking time.

- Once the gnocchi are good to go, continue to roll out the rest of the dough and form them into individual gnocchi. Spread finished gnocchi on a floured baking sheet and place in fridge if you are going to cook them later.
- When all gnocchi are shaped, cook in batches of 20 to 30 at a time in a large pot of salted boiling water until done. Mix with sauce and serve immediately.

Sauces: You can't go wrong with an Alfredo Sauce (page 59) on these tasty gnocchi. If, however, just can't cook Italian food without tomatoes forever, a spicy Arrabiata sauce is delicious on these gnocchi.

Risotto

A staple of Northern Italian cooking, risotto is a rice dish that transcends almost all other starch dishes. Through slow careful cooking, a creamy batch of risotto can be anything from a hearty first course to a well-placed side dish to accompany any main course.

Like tomatoes, rice isn't native to Italy. So how did this imported grain, which the Italians have so adeptly infused into their cuisine, get to Italy in the first place? Rice was introduced by the Arabs when they conquered Sicily and were trading heavily with the southern parts of the Italian mainland in the late Middle Ages. But it was in the marshlands of the Po River valley, far in the north of Italy, where rice really took hold.

Thus, risotto is recognized as a cornerstone of northern Italian cooking. In states like Veneto, Piemonte, and Lombardia, risotto is often served in place of pasta, and rightfully so. The rich, creamy consistency of risotto can be made by anyone who learns the simple steps to proper risotto making.

That process begins not only with good rice (Carnaroli and Arborio being my two favorites), but with good broth as well. Here in America, our broth is much stronger than the broth they use in Italy, so you'll have to dilute your broth when making risotto. If you use full strength American broth to make risotto, you'll end up with concentrated flavors that are too overpowering; so, in these risotto recipes, the liquids used are half broth and half water.

Once you get the hang of the steps and procedure involved in making risotto, you're sure to be inventing your own recipes and enjoying this most sublime rice dish for any occasion.

Basic Risotto

This is a useful template for risotto that will provide you with a base for almost any topping. You can apply the fundamentals of what you learn here to any risotto recipe, and it should come out perfect every time.

The first real trick to making perfect risotto is to make sure you add the broth slowly. Add more liquid only when almost all of the previous addition of liquid has been absorbed by the rice. Secondly, you need to incorporate some sort of fat into the risotto at the end. The Italian name for this step is *mantecato* ("creamy"), which gives risotto its amazingly creamy texture.

Simply put, the cooking technique of risotto creates a network of starch between the grains of rice, and takes advantage of this network to incorporate some creamy butter, delicious cheese, or flavorful oil into the dish. Proper technique is what will take your risotto to the next level.

Serves 4

1¾ cups Chicken Stock (page 173) or vegetable broth

1¾ cups water

2 Tablespoons unsalted butter

1 small onion – finely diced

2 cloves garlic – minced

1 cup risotto rice – Arborio or Carnaroli

½ cup dry white wine

Kosher salt

Freshly ground black pepper

4 Tablespoons butter and/or ½ cup freshly grated *Parmigiano Reggiano* – to finish

- In a medium saucepan, heat stock and water to a gentle simmer over medium-high heat. Reduce heat to low to keep warm.
- In a large saucepan, melt butter over medium heat. Add onions and sauté until translucent.
- Add garlic; cook until fragrant, about 30 seconds.
- Add rice and cook briefly, stirring until all grains are coated with butter, about 1 minute.
- Add wine and stir until it is completely absorbed by rice.
- Add stock to risotto, 1 to 2 ladlefuls at a time. Stirring occasionally, cook until stock is almost completely absorbed into the risotto before adding any more stock. When you can drag your spoon across the bottom of the pan and make a line that does not collapse instantly, you can add the next ladleful of stock. Repeat until stock is absorbed, and rice is tender, but not mushy.
- Remove risotto from heat, and add butter and/or cheese to create a creamy consistency (if you want to add more, that's just fine!). Taste and adjust seasonings.
- Serve immediately while hot as a side for almost any meat dish, or top with any accompaniment as a first course. For an example of how to use Basic Risotto, see the next recipe.

BRAISED CHICKEN RISOTTO WITH MUSHROOMS AND ZUCCHINI

I use leg pieces for this recipe because I think they are more flavorful, and they tend to braise better than breasts. But if you are a white meat chicken person, you can use two chicken breasts in this recipe instead.

Serves 4-6

1 ounce dried porcini mushrooms

½ cup warm water

2 Tablespoons vegetable oil

3 ounces pancetta – thinly sliced and cut into strips

Kosher salt

Freshly ground black pepper

2 chicken legs – separated into thighs and drumsticks, patted dry with paper towels

6 ounces cremini mushrooms – sliced

½ zucchini – sliced very thin

2 cloves garlic – minced

1 cup medium-bodied red wine (Sangiovese or Chianti)

1 sprig fresh rosemary – left whole

1 Tablespoon fresh thyme – minced

3 bay leaves

1 recipe Basic Risotto (page 85)

- Line a plate with paper towels and set aside.
- In a medium bowl, soak porcinis in warm water for about ½ hour. Reserving soaking liquid, transfer porcinis to a small bowl. Set aside porcinis and soaking liquid separately.
- Heat oil in a large skillet over medium heat. Add pancetta and cook until it is crispy and most of its fat has been rendered. Remove pancetta to the lined plate and set aside.
- Sprinkle salt and pepper on chicken. Increase heat to medium-high, add chicken pieces to the pan, and brown on all sides. Remove from the pan to a separate plate and set aside.
- Reduce heat to medium, remove all but 2 Tablespoons of the fat from the pan. Add cremini mushrooms, zucchini, garlic and reserved porcinis to the pan. Cook until mushrooms and zucchini are browning nicely, about 2 minutes.
- Add wine to the pan along with the reserved soaking water from the porcinis. Bring the mixture to a boil while scraping up any browned bits from the bottom of the pan. Allow mixture to boil for about 1 minute.
- Reduce heat to medium-low and keep liquid at a simmer. Add rosemary, thyme, and bay leaves. Return chicken and any accumulated juices to the pan and simmer, covered, until chicken is falling-off-the-bone tender, about 1 hour.

- When chicken has been cooking for 30 minutes, begin making Basic Risotto.
- When chicken is done, remove it to a cutting board. Pull meat off bones, and shred it using two forks, or your hands if it is cool enough. Remove and discard bay leaves and rosemary sprig. Add shredded chicken back to sauce.
- Serve finished Basic Risotto covered with braised chicken mixture, and top that with reserved pancetta.

RISOTTO WITH PANCETTA AND ASPARAGUS

Hearty Italian bacon, known as pancetta, pairs beautifully with the fresh, crisp taste of asparagus to make a risotto that can't be beat. If you can't find pancetta, American bacon is the closest substitute; though there is a smoky flavor in bacon that pancetta doesn't have.

Serves 4-6

1 pound fresh thin asparagus

3 Tablespoons extra virgin olive oil – divided

Kosher salt

Freshly ground black pepper

2½ cups Chicken Stock (page 173)

2½ cups water

¼ pound thickly sliced pancetta or bacon – cut into 1-inch pieces

½ onion – small dice

2 cloves garlic – minced

1½ cups risotto rice – Arborio or Carnaroli

½ cup dry white wine

¼-½ cup freshly grated *Parmigiano Reggiano*

- Preheat your oven's broiler, or if your oven doesn't have a broiler, preheat oven to 450° F. Line a rimmed baking sheet with foil.

- Snap off tough ends from asparagus spears, and peel stalks if desired.

- Brush asparagus with 2 Tablespoons olive oil and season with salt and pepper to taste. Arrange asparagus on prepared baking sheet.

- Broil or roast asparagus spears in the oven until lightly browned on all sides. Remove from oven and cut into 2-inch lengths.

- In a medium saucepan over medium heat, bring stock and water to a light simmer. Reduce heat to low and keep stock warm.

- Line a plate with paper towels and set aside.

- In a large saucepan, heat remaining 1 Tablespoon olive oil over medium-high heat and add pancetta. (Omit oil if using bacon.) Cook until done, but still tender. Remove pancetta and set aside on lined plate.

- Using the fat in the pan, cook onions until translucent. Add garlic and cook until fragrant, about 30 seconds.

- Add rice and stir constantly for about 1 minute until rice is translucent.

- Add wine to the rice, and cook, stirring continually, until it is absorbed completely.

- Add stock to risotto, 1 to 2 ladlefuls at a time. Stirring occasionally, cook until it is almost completely absorbed into the risotto before adding any more stock. When you can drag your spoon across the bottom of the pan and make a line that does not collapse instantly, you can add the next ladleful of stock. Repeat until stock is absorbed, and rice is tender, but not mushy.

- When rice is done, remove from heat. Stir in the reserved asparagus and pancetta, as well as Parmesan and some freshly ground pepper to taste. Serve immediately.

SEAFOOD RISOTTO

A great use for a variety of seafood, this risotto works as well with fresh seafood as it does with frozen. If you are using frozen cooked seafood, leave out the step of cooking the shrimp and mussels and start with the cooking of the risotto.

Serves 4-6

3 cups Seafood Stock (page 174)

Kosher salt

½ pound shrimp (20-24 count is the size I recommend) – peeled and deveined

20-25 mussels – in shells

1 leek – white and light green part only

6 Tablespoons unsalted butter – divided

½ medium white onion – finely diced

2 cloves garlic – minced

1 cup risotto rice – Arborio or Carnaroli

½ cup white wine

3 tubes calamari – cleaned and thinly sliced

3 Tablespoons vodka

Freshly ground black pepper

1 Tablespoon fresh lemon juice

2 Tablespoons fresh parsley – for garnish

- In a medium saucepan over medium-high heat, bring stock, 1 cup water, and 2 Tablespoons salt to a light boil.
- Prepare an ice bath by filling a large bowl with ice cubes and cold water. Set aside.
- Add shrimp to the stock and cook for 3 minutes. With a slotted spoon, remove shrimp to the ice bath to cool.
- Add mussels to the stock, and cook, covered, for about 2 minutes until mussels open their shells. With a slotted spoon, remove mussels to the ice bath with shrimp to cool. Reserve stock.
- When shrimp and mussels are cooled, remove mussels from shells and set cooked shrimp and mussels aside on a plate in the fridge while finishing the risotto. Discard ice bath.
- Measure stock and add enough water to bring it to a total of 4 cups in volume. Keep stock warm over low heat.
- Slice leek in half lengthwise and wash out any dirt between the layers.
- Thinly slice white and light green parts of the leek crosswise into thin semicircles. Set the white and light green parts of the leek aside separately.

- In a separate saucepan, melt 2 Tablespoons butter, and sauté white part of the leek together with the onions until translucent.
- Add garlic, sauté until fragrant, about 30 seconds.
- Add rice and cook briefly, stirring until all grains are coated with butter and shiny, about 1 minute.
- Add the wine, cook until absorbed by rice.
- Add stock to risotto, 1 to 2 ladlefuls at a time. Stirring occasionally, cook until it is almost completely absorbed into the risotto before adding any more stock. When you can drag your spoon across the bottom of the pan and make a line that does not collapse instantly, you can add the next ladleful of stock.
- Continue in this manner until only 1 ladleful of stock remains in the medium saucepan.
- Add shrimp, mussels, and calamari rings to risotto; and cook for 2 minutes.
- Add vodka and cook for 30 seconds.
- Add remaining stock; cook until absorbed by rice. Make sure rice is cooked through and tender, but not mushy. Season to taste with salt and pepper.
- Remove risotto from heat, add remaining 4 Tablespoons butter and reserved light green part of leek.
- Stir in fresh lemon juice and garnish with parsley. Serve immediately.

Brown Butter and Cauliflower Risotto with Almonds and Hot Peppers

A lovely head of cauliflower can be used in so many dishes. It can be hard to come up with a dish that explodes with flavor, yet doesn't mask the subtle flavors of the cauliflower. This dish does just that. For an extra boost of cauliflower flavor, I cook the cauliflower stems that would otherwise be discarded in the broth for a brief while.

Serves 4-6

½ head cauliflower – cut into small florets, thick stem pieces removed and reserved

7 Tablespoons butter – divided

5 teaspoons sliced almonds

2 cherry peppers (or 1 red jalapeño pepper) – seeded and sliced

¼ teaspoon crushed red pepper

2 Tablespoons Oven-Roasted Prosciutto (page 183)

1¾ cups Chicken Stock (page 173)

2 cups water

1 small onion – finely diced

2 cloves garlic – minced

1 cup risotto rice – Arborio or Carnaroli

½ cup dry white wine

¼ cup freshly grated *Parmigiano Reggiano*

¼ cup Gorgonzola Dolce

Kosher salt

Freshly ground black pepper

2 scallions – thinly sliced on the diagonal, for garnish

- Prepare an ice bath by filling a large bowl with ice cubes and cold water. Set aside.
- Bring a large pot of salted water to a boil. Add cauliflower florets and cook until tender, about 5 minutes. Drain cauliflower and place in the ice bath to stop cooking. When cauliflower is cool, drain, and set aside. Discard ice bath.
- Heat a large skillet over medium-high heat. Add 3 Tablespoons butter, and cook until it begins to brown. Add almonds and cook briefly until fragrant, about 30 seconds. Add cooked cauliflower florets and cook well until browned lightly. Add cherry peppers and crushed red pepper, and remove from heat. Add Oven Roasted Prosciutto and stir in thoroughly. Set aside.

- In a medium saucepan, heat Chicken Stock and water over medium-high heat and add reserved cauliflower stems. Simmer for 10 minutes, and then discard stems. Keep stock warm on stove over low heat.

- In a large saucepan, melt 2 Tablespoons butter over medium heat; add onions and sauté until translucent. Add garlic, cook until fragrant, about 30 seconds.

- Add rice and cook briefly, stirring until all grains are coated with butter, about 1 minute.

- Stir in white wine and cook until completely absorbed.

- Add stock to risotto 1 to 2 ladlefuls at a time. Stirring occasionally, cook until it is almost completely absorbed into the risotto before adding any more stock. When you can drag your spoon across the bottom of the pan and make a line that does not collapse instantly, you can add the next ladleful of stock. Repeat until stock is absorbed, and rice is tender, but not mushy.

- When rice is finished, remove from heat. Add remaining 2 Tablespoons butter, Parmesan, Gorgonzola, and the cauliflower mixture. Stir until thoroughly combined.

- Season to taste with salt and pepper. Serve immediately, garnished with scallions.

BUTTERNUT SQUASH AND ESCAROLE RISOTTO

This is a fabulous dish which brings together some of my favorite flavors: squash, escarole, hazelnuts, and goat cheese. I reserve a handful of the escarole to add at the end to have some escarole with more "body"; but alternatively you could sauté the reserved escarole in brown butter and serve it on top with some extra grated *Parmigiano Reggiano*.

Serves 4-6

1 small butternut squash

1 small stick cinnamon

2½ cups Chicken Stock (page 173) or vegetable broth

2½ cups water

4 Tablespoons olive oil – divided

1 small onion – sliced

Kosher salt

1½ cups risotto rice – Arborio or Carnaroli

½ cup dry white wine

⅓ pound escarole – rinsed, drained, and coarsely chopped, divided

¼ cup chopped hazelnuts

4 ounces goat cheese – crumbled

½ cup freshly grated *Parmigiano Reggiano* – plus extra for garnish

Freshly ground black pepper

Special equipment needed: 100% cotton cheesecloth and kitchen twine

- Peel and halve squash. Remove seeds and reserve. Cut flesh into ½-inch cubes and set aside 1½ cups. Reserve any additional squash for another recipe. Wrap and tie squash seeds and fibers and cinnamon stick in a piece of cheesecloth.

- In a medium saucepan over medium heat, heat stock, water, and the sachet of squash seeds in cheesecloth until lightly simmering. Reduce heat to low and keep warm.

- In a large saucepan, heat 1 Tablespoon olive oil over medium heat. Sauté onions until translucent.

- Add squash cubes, ½ cup water, and a generous pinch of salt. Cover and cook over medium-low heat until squash is tender, about 10 to 15 minutes. Remove lid from pan, increase heat to medium, and allow most of the remaining liquid to evaporate.

- Add rice to the pan and cook, stirring until translucent, about 2 minutes.

- Stir in white wine and cook until completely absorbed.

- Add most of the escarole (reserve one handful), stir to combine.

- Add stock to risotto 1 to 2 ladlefuls at a time. Stirring occasionally, cook until it is almost completely absorbed into the risotto before adding any more stock. When you can drag your spoon across the bottom of the pan and make a line that does not collapse instantly, you can add the next ladleful of stock.
- Before adding the last ladleful of stock, add hazelnuts and stir to combine.
- Add remaining ladleful of stock, and cook until rice is finished. When rice is *al dente*, remove from the heat, add remaining 3 Tablespoons olive oil, goat cheese, Parmesan, and reserved handful of escarole. Season to taste with salt and pepper.
- Serve immediately, and pass extra Parmesan at the table.

LEEK AND PORCINI RISOTTO WITH WHITE TRUFFLE OIL

The idea for this risotto was introduced to me by an incredibly talented French chef I worked with. Since he isn't Italian, his version used shiitake mushrooms. For authenticity's sake, I favor porcinis, but if you prefer to try this risotto with shiitakes, it works just fine. Fresh porcinis would also be great here if you can find them. When adding the white truffle oil at the end, remember that it is both a powerful flavor and an expensive ingredient, so add it slowly and taste between additions!

Serves 4-8

1 ounce dried porcini mushrooms

2 leeks – white and light green parts only

¾ cup heavy cream

Kosher salt

Freshly ground black pepper

2½ cups vegetable broth

2½ cups water

2 Tablespoons unsalted butter

1 onion – diced

2 cloves garlic – minced

1½ cups risotto rice – Arborio or Carnaroli

½ cup dry white wine

½ cup freshly grated *Parmigiano Reggiano* – plus extra for garnish

¼ cup chopped fresh flat leaf parsley

1-2 teaspoons white truffle oil – to finish

- Soak porcinis in 1 cup hot water for 30 minutes. Remove porcinis from water and chop coarsely. Set aside.

- Slice leeks in half lengthwise and wash out any dirt between the layers. Slice leeks crosswise into thin semicircles.

- Bring leeks and cream to a boil in a medium saucepan over medium-high heat. Reduce heat to medium and simmer, stirring occasionally, until leeks are tender, about 15 minutes. Season to taste with salt and pepper. Set aside.

- Heat broth and water in a small saucepan over low heat and keep warm.

- Heat butter in a large saucepan over medium-high heat. Add onions and cook until translucent. Add garlic, and cook until fragrant, about 30 seconds.

- Add rice, and cook briefly, stirring until all grains are coated with butter, about 1 minute.

- Add wine, and stir until it is completely absorbed by the rice.

- Add broth to risotto 1 to 2 ladlefuls at a time. Stirring occasionally, cook until it is almost completely absorbed into the risotto before adding any more broth. When you can drag your spoon across the bottom of the pan and make a line that does not collapse instantly, you can add the next ladleful of broth. Repeat until broth is absorbed, and rice is tender, but not mushy.

- When the risotto is done, add reserved mushrooms, and cook until mushrooms are heated through, about 1 minute.

- Remove risotto from heat, and add the leek and cream mixture as well as the Parmesan and parsley. Season to taste with salt and pepper.

- Stir in truffle oil, ½ teaspoon at a time, tasting between each addition until the desired flavor is reached.

- Serve immediately, garnished with extra Parmesan.

Pear and Radicchio Risotto with Red Grapes

Who says a risotto has to contain only savory elements? You can easily add fresh fruit to a creamy risotto and come up with something truly delicious. This risotto combines flavors, colors, and textures in a way that will surprise everyone you serve it to. It's not a dessert – but it's still likely to be everyone's favorite course.

Serves 4-6

2½ cups vegetable broth

2½ cups water

4 Tablespoons unsalted butter – divided

1 small onion – finely diced

1½ cups risotto rice – Arborio or Carnaroli

½ cup dry white wine

1 Anjou or Bartlett pear – unpeeled

½ head radicchio – rinsed and drained, very thinly sliced, divided

4 ounces red seedless grapes – halved

½ cup coarsely chopped walnuts – toasted

3 Tablespoons freshly grated *Parmigiano Reggiano*

3 Tablespoons mascarpone

2 ounces Gorgonzola Dolce – rind removed, at room temperature

Kosher salt

Freshly ground black pepper

- In a medium saucepan over medium-high heat, heat broth and water to a gentle simmer, then reduce heat to low to keep warm.
- In a large saucepan over medium heat, melt 2 Tablespoons butter. Add onions and sauté until translucent.
- Add rice and cook briefly, stirring until all grains are coated with butter, about 1 minute.
- Add wine, and stir until it is completely absorbed by rice.
- Add broth to risotto, 1 to 2 ladlefuls at a time. Stirring occasionally, cook until it is almost completely absorbed into the risotto before adding any more broth. When you can drag your spoon across the bottom of the pan and make a line that does not collapse instantly, you can add the next ladleful of broth. Repeat until broth is absorbed, and rice is tender, but not mushy.
- While the risotto is cooking, melt remaining 2 Tablespoons butter in a medium skillet over medium heat. Slice pear into quarters, cut out the core, and cut each quarter into 4 pieces for a total of 16 pieces. Sauté pear slices in the butter until softened and golden. Keep warm while risotto finishes.

- When the risotto is cooked, reserve a handful of radicchio for garnish, and stir the rest of radicchio into the risotto along with grapes and walnuts.
- Remove risotto from the heat and add Parmesan, mascarpone, and Gorgonzola Dolce. Stir until combined and creamy.
- Stir in half of the cooked pears. Taste and correct for salt and pepper.
- To serve, portion out risotto onto plates and garnish with remaining pears and reserved radicchio.

Risotto Milanese Arancine

The base of these wonderful fried risotto balls is the traditional Risotto Milanese – risotto with saffron. You can stop the recipe there, and have a perfectly prepared traditional risotto dish, and the quintessential base for Osso Bucco. But if you want a real treat, roll the risotto into balls, stuff them with fresh mozzarella, and fry them into a treat called *arancine* – "little oranges."

Makes 40-50 small *arancine*

¾ teaspoon saffron threads

2½ cups plus 1 Tablespoon water – divided

2½ cups Chicken Stock (page 173)

3 Tablespoons unsalted butter

1 onion – finely diced

1½ cups risotto – Arborio or Carnaroli

¾ cup dry white wine

¾ cup freshly grated *Parmigiano Reggiano*

Kosher salt

Freshly ground black pepper

4-6 cups vegetable oil – for frying

1 large egg yolk

½ pound fresh mozzarella – preferably buffalo milk, cut into 40-50 (½-inch) cubes

1 cup dry bread crumbs

- In a small bowl, combine saffron threads and 1 Tablespoon water. Set aside.
- In a medium saucepan over medium-high heat, heat stock and remaining 2½ cups water to a gentle simmer. Reduce heat to low to keep warm.
- Melt butter in a large saucepan over medium heat and sauté onions until translucent.
- Add rice and cook briefly, stirring until all grains are coated with butter, about 1 minute.
- Add wine, and stir until completely absorbed by rice.
- Add stock to risotto 1 to 2 ladlefuls at a time. Stirring occasionally, cook until it is almost completely absorbed into the risotto before adding any more stock. When you can drag your spoon across the bottom of the pan and make a line that does not collapse instantly, you can add the next ladleful of stock. Repeat until stock is absorbed, and rice is tender, but not mushy.
- (If you are going to continue with the *arancine*, be sure extra moisture is well-cooked out of the risotto. If the risotto is too moist, it won't be able to roll into a ball and hold its shape.)
- Add reserved saffron, and its soaking water. Stir to combine.
- Off the heat, stir in Parmesan. Season with salt and pepper to taste.

Note: At this point, you have now created a perfect Risotto Milanese. You can serve this as is. To make the *arancine*, continue with the recipe.

- Heat frying oil in deep fryer or a large saucepan on the stove to 350° F. (If using a saucepan, make sure the oil is deep enough for the *arancine* to be completely submerged.)
- Place risotto in a large bowl and allow to cool for 10 minutes. Stir in egg yolk.
- If necessary, pat mozzarella cubes dry with a paper towel.
- Take a piece of risotto, about the size of a ping-pong ball, and tuck a piece of mozzarella inside. Shape risotto into a ball.
- Roll risotto ball in bread crumbs to coat evenly. Continue rolling until all the risotto is used up making *arancine*.
- Line a plate with paper towels. Fry the *arancine* in small batches of 5 to 8 until golden, about 1 to 1½ minutes. Remove to the lined plate to drain well, and serve hot.

Note: If you are making the *arancine* for a party (as well you should!) you can roll all of the stuffed risotto balls ahead of time, and keep them cool on a baking sheet in your fridge. When your guests arrive, continue with the recipe by rolling the balls in bread crumbs and frying them in batches.

Risotto with Gorgonzola Dolce and Spinach

Cheeses melt into risotto so smoothly – and this soft, northern Italian cheese is a perfect selection for this richly flavored risotto.

Serves 6-8

3½ cups Chicken Stock (page 173) or vegetable broth

3½ cups water

3 Tablespoons unsalted butter

1 medium onion – diced

2 cloves garlic – minced

2 cups risotto rice – Arborio or Carnaroli

½ cup dry white wine

8 ounces fresh baby spinach leaves – rinsed and dried

½-¾ cup Gorgonzola Dolce – rind removed, at room temperature

¾ cup freshly grated *Parmigiano Reggiano* – plus extra for garnish

½ teaspoon ground nutmeg

1½ teaspoons minced fresh thyme

Kosher salt

Freshly ground black pepper

- In a medium saucepan over medium heat, bring stock and water to a light simmer. Reduce heat to low and keep stock warm.
- In a large saucepan over medium-high heat, melt butter. Add onions, cook until translucent.
- Add garlic, cook until fragrant, about 30 seconds.
- Add rice and sauté for 1 minute, or until the grains are also translucent.
- Add wine and cook, stirring continually, until it is absorbed completely.
- Add stock to risotto, 1 to 2 ladlefuls at a time. Stirring occasionally, cook until stock is almost completely absorbed into the risotto before adding any more stock. When you can drag your spoon across the bottom of the pan and make a line that does not collapse instantly, you can add the next ladleful of stock.
- Continue adding stock until approximately 2 ladlefuls remain in the small saucepan.
- Add spinach to the risotto. Wait for the spinach leaves to give off their water, and wait for that water to be absorbed by the rice.
- Finish cooking rice by adding the final ladlefuls of stock. Test to make sure the rice is *al dente*.
- Remove pot from heat, and add Gorgonzola, Parmesan, nutmeg, and thyme. Stir until the cheeses are absorbed. Season to taste with salt and pepper.
- Serve in individual bowls and with extra Parmesan at the table.

Polenta

Polenta's origins are, like risotto, from the northern parts of Italy, where the majority of the country's corn is grown. Like tomatoes, corn is also an import that came to Italy after the discovery of the New World. The great chefs of Italy were able to use this new crop in innovative ways and make it such a staple part of their cuisine that it is hard to believe that corn was not always a part of their culinary heritage.

It used to be that polenta was merely a peasant dish because it was so simple to make and was generally affordable. But recently chefs have begun to embrace not only the wholesome simplicity of polenta but also its amazing versatility. Polenta can be served like a creamy risotto, topped with any number of accompanying sauces; or it can be formed into loaves, sliced and then pan-fried, grilled, or even deep-fried. You can even spread it out thinly on baking sheets and make polenta sheets that can be used in a lasagna! It really can be used as the starch in almost any dish.

The fact that polenta has all but left its humble origins behind and is now a favorite of top-level chefs means that the price has increased accordingly. At the end of the day, polenta is coarsely ground cornmeal, which we in the United States know better as "grits." When shopping for polenta, compare the price of a bag of polenta to a similar bag of grits, and you'll see an easy way to save yourself some money. For appearance sake, however, you'll probably want to use yellow (instead of white) cornmeal. It just looks more "Italian" that way.

The core of it all is the proper cooking of polenta. I've read hundreds of cookbooks; each one has a different way of making polenta. I have tried them all, and while most of them produce a fine end product, many of them involve way too much work and/or dishes. Out of these hundreds of batches of polenta I've made over the years, I've come up with what I consider to be the easiest way to make the best polenta. As with the risotto, my Basic Polenta (page 105) serves as the base for any variations of polenta, some simple examples of which I offer up here.

BASIC POLENTA

This is where it all begins, and it's much easier than you'd think. The only catch is that polenta has to cook for about 30 to 40 minutes – there's just no way around it. The only way to shorten that time is to use "instant" polenta, but there is no way I'm an advocate for that. The best part of this recipe is its simplicity. You can start the polenta, and have it be cooking away while you work on the other parts of the recipes that follow.

Serves 4-6

½ cup heavy cream

½ cup milk

2 cups water

3 sprigs fresh thyme

1 shallot – peeled and coarsely chopped

2 cloves garlic – peeled and smashed

2 bay leaves

1 teaspoon whole black peppercorns

1 cup polenta

Kosher salt

Special equipment needed: 100% cotton cheesecloth and kitchen twine

- Combine cream, milk, and water in a large saucepan, heat over medium heat.

- Combine thyme, shallots, garlic, bay leaves, and peppercorns in a cheesecloth sachet, and tie it off with kitchen twine. Add the sachet to the saucepan.

- When cream mixture is warmed and beginning to steam, slowly pour in polenta while stirring continually to keep any lumps from forming. The total pouring time should be about 20 to 30 seconds.

- Cook polenta at a very light simmer (one bubble every 2 seconds), stirring occasionally until polenta is cooked through. Polenta is done when it both pulls away from the sides of the pan when it is stirred and is no longer gritty. This will take about 30 to 40 minutes. Add more water, if necessary, while it is cooking to keep the consistency creamy.

- Remove cheesecloth sachet, and squeeze out any juice into the polenta. Stir juice into polenta and discard sachet.

- Season with salt to taste.

At this point, the polenta can be served. Topped with a little Parmesan, it is a perfect side dish! It is also ready to be used in all the other dishes that follow.

POLENTA WITH THREE CHEESES AND WILD MUSHROOM SAUTÉ

This dish is as hearty as it is rich. There is just no way to praise the blending of these three great cheeses enough. Matching them with a collection of mushrooms – well, that is Northern Italian cooking at its finest. This dish is great for company, or just when you need some warming comfort food.

Serves 4-6

1 ounce dried porcini mushrooms

3 cups hot water

1 recipe Basic Polenta (page 105), made with 3 cups water from soaking mushrooms only, no milk or cream

Kosher salt

Freshly ground black pepper

2 Tablespoons olive oil

2 cloves garlic – minced

1 sprig fresh rosemary – leaves only, chopped

2 sprigs fresh thyme – leaves only, chopped

¼ cup chopped fresh flat leaf parsley

¼ cup dry white wine

6 ounces wild mushrooms (shiitake, oyster, chanterelles, or any mixture of these) – trimmed and sliced

½ pound cremini or white button mushrooms – trimmed and sliced

¼ pound Gorgonzola Dolce – rind removed, cut into chunks

½ pound Fontina – shredded

½ cup freshly grated *Parmigiano Reggiano* – plus extra for garnish

- In a large bowl, soak porcini mushrooms in hot water for 20 minutes. Remove mushrooms; strain and reserve soaking liquid. Coarsely chop mushrooms. Set aside mushrooms and soaking liquid separately.

- Make a single recipe of the Basic Polenta, but use the porcini mushroom soaking liquid to cook the polenta instead of any milk or cream.

- While polenta is cooking, begin the mushroom sauté. Heat olive oil in a large skillet over medium heat. Add garlic and cook until fragrant, about 30 seconds.

- Add herbs and cook until fragrant, another 30 seconds.

- Add wine and deglaze the pan by bringing the mixture to a boil while scraping up any browned bits from the bottom of the pan. Cook until the pan is almost dry.

- Add wild mushroom mixture, cremini mushrooms, and reserved porcini mushrooms to the pan. Cook until mushrooms have released all their liquid and are browning nicely. Taste and adjust seasonings.

- When the polenta is done, stir in the three cheeses until they are completely melted. Season to taste with salt and pepper.
- If you've timed it right, the polenta and mushrooms should be complete at about the same time. Serve the polenta in bowls topped with the mushroom sauté and some extra grated Parmesan.

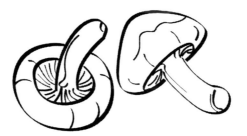

Fried Polenta with Sausages and Peppers

Pan-frying the polenta is a great way to enhance this dish since you get the crispy exterior and the creamy inside. The trick is to make sure you coat the outside of the polenta blocks with some cornmeal to keep them from sticking to the bottom of the pan. I wouldn't use more polenta (coarse ground cornmeal) for the coating as those coarse grains make the final dish a little too gritty in texture. The smaller grains of fine ground cornmeal work much better.

Serves 4-6

2 recipes Basic Polenta (page 105)

1 cup grated fontina cheese

Fine ground cornmeal – for dusting

Vegetable oil – for frying

2 Tablespoons olive oil

¾-1 pound sweet Italian sausage (or Homemade Sausages – page 142)

2 cloves garlic – halved

3 green bell peppers – cut into ¾-inch wide strips

Kosher salt

Freshly ground black pepper

2 Tablespoons Balsamic Reduction (page 182)

¼ cup sliced fresh basil

- Line a rimmed baking sheet with parchment paper and thoroughly grease a large loaf pan. Set both aside.

- Make a double recipe of Basic Polenta. When the polenta is finished, melt in fontina. Pour polenta into the prepared loaf pan, and place in refrigerator until set, about 2 hours.

- Remove polenta from loaf pan and slice into 1-inch thick slices. Dust each slice on both sides lightly with cornmeal and place in a single layer on the prepared baking sheet. Set aside.

- Preheat oven to 200° F. Line a separate rimmed baking sheet with paper towels.

- Heat about ⅓-inch vegetable oil in a large skillet over medium heat. When oil is shimmering, gently lay polenta slices into oil and fry until crispy and brown on each side, about 3 minutes per side. Place finished polenta on the prepared baking sheet and keep warm in the oven.

- Continue frying the rest of the polenta slices, and keep all finished slices warm in the oven.

- While you are frying the polenta, heat olive oil in a separate large skillet over medium heat. Add sausages and cook until done, about 5 minutes. When cooked, remove sausages from the pan, and slice on the diagonal. Place on a plate and keep warm in the oven.

- Add garlic to hot oil in the pan where you cooked sausages. Cook over medium heat until golden brown; discard garlic.

- Line a plate with paper towels. Add peppers to the hot garlic oil, enough to cover bottom of the pan in a single layer – don't overcrowd the pan. Increase heat to medium-high, and cook until browned nicely on both sides, about 3 to 4 minutes per side. Remove to the lined plate; season with salt and pepper to taste. If you need to cook the peppers in batches, keep first batch of peppers warm in oven while you cook the second batch.
- When the peppers are all cooked, assemble the final dish: Create a ring of sausages and peppers on each plate, or on a large serving plate, and place the fried polenta in the middle. Drizzle on the Balsamic Reduction and garnish with fresh basil. Serve immediately.

Note: Fried polenta is the perfect complement to the Wild Mushroom Sauté (page 106), as well as the Garlic-Sautéed Rapini (page 122).

GRILLED POLENTA WITH FRESH CORN AND PEPPERS

This recipe is midsummer dream come true: cook this on the grill as your vegetable side dish to accompany the meat you're grilling. The results are of course best when you use fresh seasonal corn right off the cob.

Serves 4-6

1 recipe Basic Polenta (page 105)

1 Tablespoon olive oil

½ red onion – finely diced

1 clove garlic – minced

1 ear fresh corn kernels (about ¾ cup)

1 small zucchini – finely diced

½ red bell pepper – finely diced

Kosher salt

Freshly ground black pepper

Vegetable oil

Fine ground cornmeal – for dusting

1 Tablespoon white wine vinegar

½ cup freshly grated *Parmigiano Reggiano*

2 Tablespoons fresh chives – coarsely chopped

Extra virgin olive oil

- Grease a 1½-quart loaf pan.
- Prepare 1 recipe of Basic Polenta.
- While polenta is cooking, heat olive oil in a large skillet over medium heat.
- Add onions to oil, sauté briefly, about 3 minutes, until translucent but still has some color. Add garlic and cook until fragrant, about 30 seconds.
- Add corn, zucchini, and peppers. Sauté until corn kernels begin to brown lightly, about 10 more minutes. Season to taste with salt and pepper. Set aside while polenta finishes cooking.
- When polenta is done, stir ⅓ cup of the corn mixture into the polenta, and season to taste. Pour the mixture into the prepared pan. Place in refrigerator until it is cooled and sliceable, about 2 hours.
- Remove polenta from loaf pan; slice into 1½-inch thick slices. Let polenta slices rest for 30 minutes to allow them to come to room temperature. Brush slices with vegetable oil on both sides, and dust each slice on both sides lightly with cornmeal.

- Heat your grill to medium-high heat and clean grill grates thoroughly. Using a paper towel held with tongs, brush grill grates with vegetable oil.

- Grill polenta slices until nicely browned and warmed through, about 2 minutes on each side. If you're doing these in batches, be sure to clean the grill and brush with additional vegetable oil between batches.

- While polenta is grilling, gently warm the remaining corn mixture in a small saucepan on the side of the grill where you are cooking the polenta. When the mixture is warm, stir in vinegar. Keep warm until polenta is done.

- Remove polenta slices from the grill and serve hot, garnished with corn mixture, Parmesan, chives, and a drizzle of extra virgin olive oil.

Polenta "Lasagna" with Zucchini and Pesto

In this recipe, I've taken the idea of layered pasta sheets in a lasagna, and turned it into sheets of polenta layered with a delicious mix of zucchini, pesto, and cheese. The resulting dish is baked like a lasagna, and the taste is outstanding. Another example of polenta's incredible versatility! You can serve it with extra *Parmigiano Reggiano* if you wish, but I think it already has enough cheese inside!

Serves 6-9

2 recipes Basic Polenta (page 105)

1 Tablespoon olive oil

1 small onion – julienned

2 medium zucchini – thinly sliced

¼ teaspoon crushed red pepper

Kosher salt

Freshly ground black pepper

1 recipe Fresh Pesto (page 55) – divided

2 cups grated scamorza cheese (or grated mozzarella) – divided

½ cup freshly grated *Parmigiano Reggiano* – divided

9 (½-inch) slices fresh mozzarella

- Preheat oven to 425° F. Thoroughly grease a 9-inch square baking pan.
- Prepare a double recipe of Basic Polenta.
- While polenta is cooking, heat olive oil in a large skillet over medium heat. Add onions, and sauté until translucent.
- Add zucchini and sauté until soft and translucent as well, about 5 minutes.
- Add crushed red pepper; toss to combine. Season to taste with salt and black pepper. Set aside.
- Spoon one-third of the polenta into the bottom of the prepared baking pan. Use the back of the spoon to even the surface out.
- Top the polenta with one-half of the zucchini mixture, one-half of the pesto, one-half of the scamorza, and one-half of the Parmesan. (Save the fresh mozzarella slices for the top!)
- Spoon in another one-third of the polenta, smooth out, and top with remaining zucchini, pesto, and grated cheeses.
- Finish lasagna off with remaining polenta, and again smooth out the top.
- Place the 9 slices of fresh mozzarella in a 3 x 3 grid on the top of the lasagna.

- Cover baking pan with foil and bake for 30 to 40 minutes. Remove foil, and set your oven to broil. Broil the lasagna briefly to lightly brown the top layer of mozzarella and polenta.
- Remove from oven, and let lasagna rest for 10 minutes.
- Cut into 9 pieces between the fresh mozzarella slices and serve immediately.

Roasted Eggplant Polenta Topped with Zucchini and Mint

Roasted eggplant is beloved all across the Mediterranean. The subtle smoky and bitter flavors combine to make a rich polenta dish that is accented with a fresh light zucchini salad on top. Is it rich and comforting or fresh and light? Can't it be both?

Serves 4-6

1 medium eggplant (about 1 pound)

4 Tablespoons extra virgin olive oil – divided, plus extra for brushing

1½ teaspoons kosher salt – divided

1 recipe Basic Polenta (page 105)

1 pound zucchini

1 Tablespoon vegetable oil

7 teaspoons thinly sliced fresh mint – divided

2 teaspoons white wine vinegar

- Preheat oven to 400° F. Line a baking sheet with parchment paper.
- Cut eggplant in half lengthwise. Brush cut sides with olive oil and season with 1 teaspoon salt. Place eggplant, cut sides down, on the prepared baking sheet. Roast eggplant until flesh is completely soft and tender, about 40 to 50 minutes. Eggplant will have collapsed. Allow to cool before handling.
- Scoop flesh of eggplant out of skins. Discard skins and place the flesh in a food processor. Turn processor on, and with blades running, slowly add 2 Tablespoons olive oil. Continue to process until thoroughly pureed. Set aside.
- Begin making one recipe of Basic Polenta.
- While polenta is cooking, slice zucchini lengthwise with a mandoline as thinly as possible. (If you don't have a mandoline, you can use a knife; just try to get long strips as thin as possible.)
- Heat vegetable oil in a large skillet over medium-high heat. Cook zucchini strips in batches, until lightly softened and browned on each side, about 3 minutes each side. Place zucchini in a small bowl and set aside.
- Whisk together remaining 2 Tablespoons extra virgin olive oil, 4 teaspoons mint, vinegar, and remaining ½ teaspoon salt. Toss zucchini with mint vinaigrette.
- When the polenta is finished cooking, stir the roasted eggplant puree into the cooked polenta.
- Serve polenta in bowls, topped with zucchini salad and garnished with remaining 3 teaspoons mint.

Verdure

Every time I go to Italy I am always astonished at, and inspired by, the beautiful rows of fresh vegetables in the farmers markets. Even in the depths of the largest cities, piazzas are transformed regularly into fields of colorful produce that astound all the senses.

Italians love their vegetables — and why shouldn't they? The agricultural traditions of Italy generate a wide variety of excellent produce, from blood oranges in the south to white asparagus in the north. From the deep, rich greens of rapini and *cavolo nero* to the bright yellow of zucchini blossoms. As a result of this incredible variety and beauty available to them, Italians often give their vegetables a more prominent role on the plate than we do here in the United States.

Italians don't hide their veggies, they celebrate them! They highlight them, adorn them, and devour them. The modern mantra of the health food movements to "decorate your plate with color" is a rule the Italians have lived by for generations. This chapter is a great starting point for you to add a little healthful Italian living to your life and menu!

ASPARAGUS VINAIGRETTE

It is hard to think of two flavors that are better paired than asparagus and vinegar. They match each other so well that this dish is the ideal way to use a nice Italian balsamic vinegar. The addition of dried cranberries adds color and sweetness, the perfect counterpoints to this fabulous combination.

Serves 4

Asparagus:

1 pound thin asparagus

3 Tablespoons extra virgin olive oil

Kosher salt

Freshly ground black pepper

Vinaigrette:

2 Tablespoons balsamic vinegar

1 shallot – minced

1 clove garlic – minced

1 teaspoon Dijon mustard

Kosher salt

Freshly ground black pepper

6 Tablespoons extra virgin olive oil

Garnish:

¼ cup dried cranberries (optional)

- Preheat your oven's broiler, or just the oven itself to 450° F.
- Snap off tough ends of asparagus spears, and peel if desired.
- Rub with olive oil and season with salt and pepper to taste. Place on a rimmed baking sheet.
- Broil or roast asparagus spears in the oven until lightly browned on all sides.
- While asparagus are cooking, make the vinaigrette. In a small bowl, combine vinegar with shallots, garlic, mustard, and a little salt and pepper.
- Slowly add olive oil while whisking to emulsify. Set vinaigrette aside.
- When asparagus are cooked, transfer to a serving plate, top spears with vinaigrette and dried cranberries. Serve immediately.

Note: If you prefer, this recipe can also be served room temperature or cold.

FRIED ZUCCHINI BLOSSOMS

The zucchini plant has both male and female flowers. The large male flowers are removed from the plant and used primarily for this preparation that is every bit as delicious as it is beautiful. The blossoms are seasonal and are usually only available for a very short time, so look for them in farmers markets in late spring and early summer.

Serves 4-6

⅔ cup flour

¾ cup club soda (or light beer)

1 teaspoon kosher salt – divided

8 ounces fresh whole milk ricotta

1 large egg yolk

⅛ teaspoon freshly grated nutmeg

¼ cup minced chives

2 Tablespoons freshly grated *Parmigiano Reggiano*

2 cups vegetable oil

24 large zucchini blossoms

24 small pieces of Pecorino Romano – each the size of a AAA battery

- Line a large plate with paper towels.

- In a medium bowl, make the batter by whisking together flour, club soda, and ½ teaspoon salt. Set aside and let batter rest for 30 minutes.

- In a small bowl, make the filling by mixing together ricotta, egg yolk, nutmeg, chives, Parmesan, and the remaining ½ tsp salt. Set filling aside.

- In a deep fryer, or large frying pan over medium-high heat, heat oil to 375° F.

- Working with one zucchini blossom at a time, place a Tablespoon of the filling in the flower, and then slide a piece of Pecorino into the flower as well. If possible, gently twist the top of the flower to help seal the filling inside.

- After stuffing 2 or 3 flowers, gently dip the stuffed blossoms into the batter to put on a light coating, and then immediately slide them – carefully so as not to splash – into the preheated oil.

- Fry them until they are crispy and lightly browned on all sides, about 2 minutes, flipping them in the oil as needed. Using a slotted spoon, remove the flowers to the prepared plate. Season lightly with salt, and serve immediately while hot.

Note: If you want to serve all of the blossoms together, you will likely have to keep them warm in a 200°F oven while you cook all the blossoms. Though in my experience, people usually dive into these as soon as they are ready!

SAUTÉED ZUCCHINI WITH CARAMELIZED ONIONS

The Italians' ability to transform zucchini into a wide variety dishes is unrivaled. This simple sauté of thinly sliced vegetables makes the perfect accompaniment for almost any meat dish, and it can be thrown together in just a few minutes.

Serves 4-6

3 medium zucchini – ends trimmed

1 large onion

1 Tablespoon olive oil

2 cloves garlic – minced

2 teaspoons lightly chopped fresh thyme

Kosher salt

Freshly ground black pepper

Freshly grated *Parmigiano Reggiano*

- Slice zucchini into thin rounds using a mandoline or with a sharp knife. Set aside.
- Slice onion into thin semicircles, set aside.
- In a large skillet, heat olive oil over medium-high heat, and add onions. Sauté until onions begin to develop a golden color, about 4 minutes.
- Add zucchini and garlic, and continue to sauté. Toss frequently at first, then less frequently once the zucchini are fully mixed with onions. Sauté until zucchini begin to soften and develop some color.
- Add thyme; toss to combine. Season with salt and a generous amount of pepper.
- When zucchini are done, transfer to a warmed serving bowl and serve immediately topped with freshly grated Parmesan.

STUFFED ZUCCHINI

This is a favorite recipe of mine because it shows my guests that I put a little effort into the accompaniment for the main course. Of course, it doesn't hurt that it looks and tastes amazing as well.

Serves 4-8

2 Tablespoons raisins

4 medium zucchini

4 Tablespoons olive oil – divided

Kosher salt

Freshly ground black pepper

1 medium red bliss potato (about 5 ounces) – cut into ½-inch cubes

1 small onion – minced

2 cloves garlic – minced

1½ Tablespoons pine nuts – toasted

1 Tablespoon chopped fresh mint – plus extra for garnish

Pinch crushed red pepper

2 Tablespoons dry white wine

¼ cup freshly grated *Parmigiano Reggiano* – divided

- Preheat oven to 400° F. Line a rimmed baking sheet with foil.

- Plump raisins by placing them in a small bowl and covering them with warm water. Let sit for 20 minutes. Drain and set raisins aside.

- Wash zucchini and cut them in half lengthwise (don't trim off the ends!). Using a small spoon, scrape out the flesh from the zucchini, leaving only a ¼-inch of flesh on the skin of zucchini. Chop the scraped-out flesh and set aside.

- Brush the cut sides of zucchini with 2 Tablespoons olive oil, and season with salt and pepper. Place them cut-side down on prepared baking sheet.

- In a bowl, toss the potato cubes with 1 Tablespoon olive oil and season with salt and pepper. Place potatoes on the baking sheet next to the zucchini, and roast zucchini and potatoes together until tender, about 10 to 12 minutes.

- While zucchini and potatoes are roasting, heat remaining 1 Tablespoon olive oil in a large skillet over medium heat. Add onions, garlic, and reserved zucchini flesh. Sauté until a little color begins to develop, about 5 minutes.

- Add reserved raisins, pine nuts, mint, and red pepper; and sauté for 2 more minutes.

- Add white wine, and scrape up any browned bits from the bottom of the pan. Cook until wine is completely evaporated, about 1 to 2 minutes.

- Remove pan from the heat, and stir in 2 Tablespoons Parmesan. Season to taste with salt and pepper and set aside.
- When zucchini and potatoes are tender, remove from oven. Using tongs, flip the zucchini shells so they are cut side up. Add potatoes to the zucchini mixture in the skillet, and stir to combine. Mound the zucchini mixture in the zucchini shells.
- Sprinkle the remaining 2 Tablespoons Parmesan evenly over the zucchini.
- Move the rack in the oven to the top level, and place stuffed zucchini back in the oven to roast until heated through and Parmesan is slightly browned, about 5 minutes. Remove from oven and garnish with mint. Serve immediately.

GARLIC-SAUTÉED RAPINI

Most of the greens that Italians prefer are quite bitter. There are two tricks to sautéing bitter greens like rapini in the Italian style. First, you need to boil the greens briefly. This helps to tenderize them, and also removes some of the harsh bitter flavors that can develop. Second, take your time in the actual sautéing of the greens. Most sautéing is done very quickly over high heat. In this recipe, we take our time to let the blanched greens absorb the flavors of the garlic and olive oil.

Serves 4

1 pound rapini (broccoli rabe) – rinsed and dried

3 Tablespoons olive oil

3 cloves garlic – minced

Kosher salt

Crushed red pepper

- Prepare rapini by removing leaves from stems. Keep leaves whole. Chop off florets, keeping them whole. Chop stems into ½-inch pieces.
- In a large pot of boiling salted water, cook stems for about 2 minutes, and then add leaves. Cook for another 5 minutes, then add florets. Cook for an additional 3 minutes and drain in a colander. Lightly press out any excess water.
- When rapini is done draining, heat olive oil in a large skillet over medium to medium-low heat.
- Add rapini and garlic, and cook, stirring frequently, for about 15 to 20 minutes, allowing the flavors to come together.
- Season to taste with salt and red pepper, and serve immediately.

Note: These greens are great as a side dish, but they are especially good served atop a batch of Basic Polenta (page 105) in place of a pasta course.

FENNELED FINGERLING POTATOES

This recipe comes from my love of simple browned potatoes cooked in butter or olive oil until they are crispy on the outside and perfectly tender inside. By adding fennel and lemon, you have a dish straight from the heart of the Italian countryside. If you want to substitute melted butter for the olive oil in this recipe, that works just as well.

Serves 4-6

2 pounds fingerling potatoes (or small Yukon Gold potatoes)

1 bulb fennel

¼ cup olive oil

1 clove garlic – minced

2 teaspoons fennel seeds

2 teaspoons kosher salt

1 teaspoon freshly ground black pepper

1-2 teaspoons lemon zest (optional)

- Preheat oven to 400° F. Line a small rimmed baking sheet with aluminum foil.
- Scrub potatoes clean, but don't peel them. Slice them in half lengthwise. If they are especially large, slice them in half lengthwise again.
- Place potatoes in a large saucepan; cover with warm water and add a few generous pinches of kosher salt. Heat on high heat until the water just begins to boil. Stir potatoes, and let cook for about two minutes. Drain potatoes thoroughly, but do not rinse. (Potatoes will not be cooked through at this point, but that's okay.)
- While potatoes are coming to a boil, remove stalks of fennel from white bulb at the point where they meet. Discard stalks, but reserve a small handful of feathery fennel fronds for garnish.
- Slice fennel bulb into thin strips. In a large bowl, mix together fennel, olive oil, garlic, fennel seeds, salt, and pepper. Place blanched potatoes in the bowl and toss to coat everything evenly.
- Recipe can be prepared ahead of time to this point and mixture can rest, covered, for up to 4 hours.
- Spread out potato mixture on the prepared baking sheet. Roast, stirring once or twice, until potatoes are browned and tender and fennel is tender, about 30 minutes.
- Season to taste with salt and pepper. Garnish with reserved fennel fronds and lemon zest, if using. Serve immediately.

STUFFED ARTICHOKES

Stuffing an artichoke takes some time, but a nice large artichoke stuffed with bread and cheese is not only a great vegetarian dish, it can also serve as a meal in itself. It can be bit of work to eat this dish, so I don't recommend it as a side – serve the artichoke as its own course with a dish of melted butter, or a Bagna Cauda (page 22).

Serves 4

4 medium globe artichokes

2-3 slices Italian bread – crusts removed

2 cloves garlic – minced

$\frac{1}{3}$ cup crumbled goat cheese

2 anchovy fillets – patted dry (optional)

$\frac{1}{3}$ cup freshly grated *Parmigiano Reggiano*

$\frac{1}{4}$ cup chopped fresh flat leaf parsley

1 teaspoon chopped fresh oregano

1 Tablespoon chopped fresh basil

Kosher salt

Freshly ground black pepper

1 small onion – sliced

1 cup dry white wine

2-3 Tablespoons extra virgin olive oil

- Cook artichokes as described on page 181. Cool the artichokes, and pull out and discard the center leaves and hairy chokes. Trim bottoms of artichokes so that they will sit upright when placed on a plate. Set the artichokes aside.

- Preheat oven to 350° F.

- In a food processor, chop up slices of Italian bread to make 1 cup fresh breadcrumbs the size of small pebbles. (If you have more than one cup bread crumbs, save extra bread crumbs for another recipe.)

- Add garlic, goat cheese, and anchovies (if using) to bread crumbs, and pulse a few more times until thoroughly combined.

- Transfer bread mixture to a medium bowl. Add Parmesan, parsley, oregano, and basil. Season to taste with salt and pepper.

- Stuff the empty centers of the artichokes with the bread mixture, dividing it evenly – and working some filling into the spaces between the outer leaves as well.

- Place the sliced onion and white wine in a glass 9-inch square baking pan, or any roasting pan that can hold the artichokes tightly. Tuck in the artichokes on top of the onions and wine. Drizzle olive oil evenly over the artichokes, and cover the pan with aluminum foil.

- Cook artichokes until warmed through, about 15 minutes.

- Discard onions and cooking liquid in the baking pan. Serve artichokes immediately.

ROASTED PORTABELLAS WITH PANCETTA & PISTACHIOS

The rich, earthy flavors of this dish are fabulous on their own, but they are also great alongside a steak or other red meat dish.

Serves 4-6

Roasted Portabellas:

4 large portabella caps

2 cloves garlic – minced

1 sprig fresh rosemary – left whole

½ cup extra virgin olive oil

⅓ cup balsamic vinegar

1 teaspoon kosher salt

½ teaspoon freshly ground black pepper

Sauté with Pancetta and Pistachios:

1 Tablespoon olive oil

3 ounces pancetta (or bacon) – thinly sliced

1 clove garlic – minced

1 shallot – minced

¼ cup coarsely chopped pistachios

3 Tablespoons dry white wine

2 Tablespoons vegetable broth

- Clean portabella caps by brushing any dirt off the top of the caps. Scrape out the black gills, and cut out the dried piece of the stem in the center. (Do not wash the mushrooms with any water!)

- In a large sealable plastic bag, combine garlic, rosemary, extra virgin olive oil, vinegar, salt, and pepper. Place portabellas in the bag with the marinade and marinate in the refrigerator for 2 to 3 hours, turning the bag over occasionally.

- When marinating is complete, preheat oven to 400° F.

- Remove caps from the bag, being sure to wipe off any excess marinade from the mushrooms. Pat each cap lightly with a paper towel to remove any excess oil from inside the caps.

- Cut off 4 aluminum foil pieces – each one large enough to encase a mushroom cap.

- Place each cap in a piece of aluminum foil, stem side up. Close the foil around the caps, and roast until the centers are tender, about 20 minutes. Open the foil and continue to roast for 5 more minutes to dry the mushrooms out slightly. Remove from oven to cool.

Note: At this stage, you now have perfectly roasted portabella caps. These make great sandwiches, or can be served on their own as a side dish. If you want the pancetta and pistachio dish, continue on with the recipe.

- When portabellas are cool enough to handle, slice each cap into ½-inch strips. Set aside.
- In large skillet, heat olive oil over medium-high heat. Add pancetta and cook until it is beginning to crisp, about 3 minutes. Remove pancetta and set aside.
- Add shallots and garlic to the pan; cook until the shallots begin to color, about 2 minutes.
- Add sliced caps, and sauté until heated through, about 2 minutes.
- Add pistachios and cook until fragrant, about 1 minute.
- Add wine and vegetable broth, and deglaze the pan by scraping up all the browned bits from the bottom of the pan.
- When all ingredients are warmed through, return the pancetta to the pan and season to taste with salt and pepper. Serve immediately.

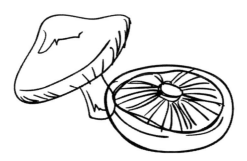

PISELLI AL GUANCIALE

At the end of the day, this dish is the well-known peas and ham. But you can make it into something so much better than what you're used to! Use fresh peas and the best quality ham you can get your hands on – the result is pure bliss. To be truly Roman, use *guanciale* (cured pork jowl) in this recipe. The results are amazing. If you can't find guanciale, use prosciutto.

Serves 3-4

¼ cup olive oil

4 ounces guanciale – in ½-inch dice (or 3 ounces prosciutto, roughly torn by hand)

1 onion – finely diced

1 pound fresh green peas

2 Tablespoons dry white wine

2 Tablespoons chopped fresh flat leaf parsley

Kosher salt

Freshly ground black pepper

- Heat olive oil in a skillet over medium-high heat.
- Add guanciale and onions, and cook until onions are tender and guanciale is becoming crispy, about 6 to 8 minutes.
- Add peas and wine. Cook, stirring continually, until peas are hot and tender, about 3 minutes.
- Drain off excess liquid, stir in parsley, season to taste with salt and pepper, and serve.

Variant: You can also heat 1½ cups cream in a large skillet over medium heat. Melt in ½ cup of freshly grated *Parmigiano Reggiano*. Pour the Piselli al Guanciale into the pan with the cream and mix together well. Heat through, and toss with 1 pound cooked penne. Garnish with chopped fresh mint and serve.

Carni/Pesce

Usually served as a separate second course after the pasta (or risotto or polenta) in Italy, the meat or fish course is usually referred to as the *secundi*. In America, we usually serve our meat alongside pastas and vegetables in one giant course, but I prefer to break the courses up.

What I really love about Italian meats is the wide variety of options that adorn a menu in a true Italian restaurant. It's not just beef, pork, and chicken, it's also duck, rabbit, and wild boar. Fresh-caught fish of all types are present, including squid, octopus, and eels. It is true that variety is the spice of life, and Italians are living life to the fullest with their incredible variety of different meat and fish dishes.

I could write an entire book (maybe several) on the meat traditions of Italy – from the humblest pork chops to the delicate salamis to the soul-satisfying braises that they always seem to get perfectly right. But that's for another time. In the meantime, this chapter provides a wide variety of ideas and introductions to Italian cooking methods and styles which, I hope, will get you experimenting more with meat in your kitchen!

One last serving note: the size of your second course should be roughly the same size as your pasta course. Plan out your dinner to so that you don't have a giant helping of food for either course so that both courses can be enjoyed – and also so you leave room for dessert!

LAMB CHOPS WITH BALSAMIC VINEGAR

Vinegar makes a great marinade; and in this simple Tuscan dish, we can see how two vinegars make the simplest of lamb dishes come alive. Serving this dish with Asparagus Vinaigrette (page 117) is not a bad idea either.

Serves 4

½ cup white wine vinegar

6 Tablespoons olive oil

1 shallot – sliced

3 sprigs fresh flat leaf parsley – chopped

1 Tablespoon whole cloves – lightly crushed

2 sprigs fresh rosemary

8 lamb rib chops

Kosher salt

Freshly ground black pepper

Balsamic vinegar for drizzling (about 2 Tablespoons)

¼ cup coarsely chopped fresh mint

½ lemon – cut into 4 wedges

- Combine white wine vinegar, olive oil, shallots, parsley, cloves, rosemary, and rib chops in a plastic bag. Let marinate in fridge, turning occasionally, for at least 1 hour or up to 4.
- Drain chops, scrape off excess marinade, and set aside.
- Heat grill to medium-high heat and clean grill grates thoroughly. Sprinkle chops with salt and pepper to taste. Cook chops to desired doneness.
- Remove chops to a serving plate, drizzle with balsamic vinegar, and garnish with mint.
- Serve lamb chops with a lemon wedge for your guests to spritz onto their chops before eating.

Steaks and Cipolline in Agrodolce

The Italian sweet and sour sauce, *agrodolce*, is beloved all over Italy – from the piazzas of Rome to the fishing towns of Sicily. Most commonly paired with onions and meat, this sauce will change how you think about steak.

Serves 4

²⁄₃ cup raisins

1 pound cipollini (or pearl) onions

4 (½-pound) strip steaks

Kosher salt

Freshly ground black pepper

3 Tablespoons olive oil

⅓ cup balsamic vinegar

5 teaspoons sugar

Vegetable oil – for brushing grill

Arugula – rinsed and dried

- Plump raisins by placing them in a small bowl and covering them with warm water. Let sit for 20 minutes. Drain and set raisins aside.
- Prepare an ice bath by filling a large bowl with ice cubes and cold water. Set aside.
- Bring a small pot of water to a boil.
- Peel onions by trimming off the root and stem ends. Run a small incision down the side of each onion. Dunk the onions (two or three at a time) in the boiling water for about 30 seconds and immediately place them in the ice bath. The skin will fall right off of the onions. Continue until all the onions are peeled. Drain and set aside.
- Preheat a grill to high heat, and then divide the fire so that you have a hot area and a cooler area.
- Pat steaks dry with paper towels. Season generously with salt and pepper. Set steaks aside.
- Heat olive oil in a large skillet over medium-high heat. Add onions; cook, stirring occasionally, until golden brown, about 8 to 10 minutes.
- Pour off excess oil from the pan; add vinegar, sugar, and reserved raisins. Season with salt. Cook, stirring continually, until sauce thickens, about 2 to 3 minutes. Raisins will remain whole – they will not break down into the sauce. Cover sauce, reduce heat to low, and keep warm while cooking steaks.
- Clean preheated grill grates thoroughly. Using a paper towel held with tongs, brush grill grates with vegetable oil.

- Sear steaks on both sides on the hot part of the grill, and then transfer them to the cooler part to cook to your desired level of doneness.
- Place steaks on a serving plate, and cover with onions and agrodolce sauce. Tent loosely with foil, and let rest 5 minutes.
- Serve steaks garnished with arugula.

BEEF IN BAROLO

This classic beef braise makes great use of one of the best wines of Northern Italy. Barolo, however, can be a rather pricey wine by the bottle. So if you want to save some money, buy a Nebbiolo or a Sangiovese. The ingredient that I find that is almost universally used with this dish is prosciutto fat. But the amount needed here can be hard to come by if you don't regularly buy whole prosciutto hams (which few of us do). So if you can't get prosciutto fat, use fatback or salt pork instead. If you're not serving this with the Fenneled Fingerling Potatoes (page 123), you're missing out.

Serves 6-8

1 (2½-pound) beef roast (chuck, sirloin, rump, or eye of round)

1 bottle Barolo wine

2 carrots – peeled and sliced

2 onions – sliced

1 stalk celery – chopped

3 cloves garlic – quartered

10 sprigs fresh flat leaf parsley

4 sprigs fresh thyme

2 sprigs fresh rosemary

2 bay leaves

1 teaspoon black peppercorns

Kosher salt

3 Tablespoons olive oil

3 Tablespoons prosciutto fat

5 Tablespoons butter – divided

Freshly ground black pepper

Special equipment needed: 100% cotton cheesecloth and kitchen twine

- If roast has parts "hanging off," you will need to tie it up with kitchen twine into an even cylindrical shape so that it is a single piece of meat that holds together. Not all roasts will need to be tied.

- Place meat in a large nonreactive container or bowl. Pour wine over meat. Add carrots, onions, and celery.

- Make your herb sachet by combining garlic, parsley, thyme, rosemary, bay leaves, and peppercorns together in the cheesecloth and tying it off with kitchen twine. Add sachet to the wine marinade, making sure the sachet is fully submerged. Stir 1 teaspoon salt into the marinade.

- Marinate beef, covered, in fridge for at least 6 hours and up to overnight.

- Reserving marinade, remove beef and pat dry with paper towels.
- In a Dutch oven, or other pan large enough to hold both roast and marinade, heat olive oil over medium-high heat. Melt in prosciutto fat and 2 Tablespoons butter. Season beef with salt and pepper, and brown on all sides in the pan.
- Add the reserved marinade, along with the vegetables and herb sachet, to the pan.
- Bring to a boil. Reduce heat to a simmer, cover pan, and cook until beef is tender, about 1½ to 2 hours.
- When the beef is almost finished cooking, preheat the oven to 200° F. Choose a serving platter that has a deep center to hold a generous amount of sauce. Place the platter in the oven to warm.
- Remove and discard the herb sachet. Remove beef to a large cutting board, and cut off the twine. Tent beef with foil while finishing sauce.
- Using an immersion blender or food mill, puree vegetables to make a thick sauce – keeping them in the Dutch oven you cooked the beef in. Reduce sauce over medium-high heat, stirring occasionally, for 5 minutes to thicken slightly. Remove sauce from heat and stir in remaining 3 Tablespoons butter.
- Pour half of the sauce into the warmed serving platter. Slice beef roast and place on top of the sauce. Serve with remaining sauce to pass at the table.

COSTOLETTE ALLA VALDOSTANA

In the northern regions of Italy, the cows are farmed throughout the mountain villages. As a result, the cheeses are wonderful; beef and veal are plentiful; and almost everything is cooked in butter. Those three elements come together in one of my favorite veal chop preparations, this fabulous dish from Val d'Aosta. Without question, you must use real Italian fontina for this recipe. The Swiss or Dutch varieties just don't cut it here.

Serves 4

4 bone-in veal chops – each about 1-1½-inches thick

4 thin slices prosciutto

4-8 thin slices Italian fontina cheese – preferably from Val d'Aosta

Kosher salt

Freshly ground black pepper

2 large eggs

2 Tablespoons milk

½ cup all purpose flour

1 cup unflavored breadcrumbs

6-8 Tablespoons butter – for frying

- Pat veal chops dry with paper towels and lay flat on a cutting board.
- Keeping veal chop flat, insert the tip of a paring knife into the side of the chop opposite the bone. Work the knife inside down to the bone, and then angle the knife side to side to create a pocket inside the cutlet without making the incision much larger than the width of the knife. Repeat for all veal chops.
- Insert prosciutto and fontina into each cutlet.
- Using the back end of a chef's knife, tap down the edges of the hole in the cutlet to seal it shut. Season chops with salt and pepper, and set aside.
- Beat eggs and milk together in a small bowl and set aside.
- Spread flour on one dinner plate and breadcrumbs on another.
- Heat a large frying pan over medium heat.
- Bread veal chops in the following manner: Dredge chops in flour, tapping off the excess; then dip chops into the egg mixture to cover, letting excess drip off; finally roll them in breadcrumbs to coat completely.
- Add butter to the preheated pan so that it melts and is frothy. Cook veal chops until golden brown and cooked through, about 5 to 7 minutes per side.
- Line a plate with paper towels.
- When chops are done, remove to the lined plate. Let rest for about 2 minutes to allow excess oil to be absorbed by the paper towels. Serve immediately.

SALT-RUBBED PORK CHOPS WITH PEACHES AND SAGE

In the world of all things culinary, there are a few flavor combinations that reign supreme: dark chocolate and raspberry; honey and almond; beef and mushroom; and (of course) tomato and basil to name a few. Try this recipe and I'm sure you'll agree that pork and peach deserves a place on this all-time great list.

Serves 4

4 (6- to 8-ounce) bone-in pork chops

3 Tablespoons kosher salt

2 Tablespoons vegetable oil

3 Tablespoons butter – divided

2 peaches – peeled, pitted, and sliced into thin wedges

1 Tablespoon honey

2 Tablespoons apple cider vinegar (or champagne vinegar)

1 teaspoon Dijon mustard

8 fresh sage leaves – coarsely chopped, plus extra leaves for garnish

Freshly ground black pepper

- Sprinkle pork chops on both sides with salt and rub the salt into the meat. Place chops on a rack on a rimmed baking sheet in the fridge, uncovered, for about 1 hour.
- Preheat oven to 200° F.
- Rinse excess salt off of pork chops, and dry completely with paper towels.
- Over medium-high heat, heat oil and 2 Tablespoons butter in a skillet that is large enough to hold all pork chops in a single layer. Reduce heat to medium. Cook pork chops in pan until both sides are nicely browned, turning only once, about 3 minutes on each side. Transfer chops to an ovenproof serving platter, cover loosely with foil, and place in the preheated oven while finishing sauce.
- Add peaches and honey to the pan used to cook the pork chops. Cook, stirring gently to coat peaches in the sauce, until peaches begin to caramelize and sauce thickens, about 2 minutes.
- Add vinegar, mustard, and chopped sage to the pan. Stir to combine, scraping up any browned bits from the bottom of the pan.
- Remove pork chops from the oven. Add any accumulated juices on the serving platter to the pan with the peaches. Stir to combine.
- Remove the skillet from the heat. Add remaining 1 Tablespoon butter to the sauce. Stir to melt in.
- Pour the peach sauce over the pork chops.
- Garnish with sage leaves and a grinding of black pepper. Serve immediately.

PORCHETTA

This dish is served all over Italy, but is especially beloved in central Italy, where it can often be found served in sandwiches. It makes a fabulous first course as well! The trick is to use a shoulder of pork with the skin, which you crisp up and serve with the porchetta. Some recipes call for a massive belly of the pig wrapped around a pork loin – but this feeds a small army. My porchetta is a more manageable size for most families, but it will still likely give you some leftovers to enjoy on Focaccia (page 176) the next day!

Serves 6-10

Note: The pork needs to marinate for 1 to 3 days.

1 (6-7 pound) boneless pork shoulder with skin still on

1½ Tablespoons kosher salt

½ Tablespoon freshly ground black pepper

1½ Tablespoons fennel seeds

5 cloves garlic – minced

1 teaspoon crushed red pepper

Zest from 1 lemon

3 sprigs fresh rosemary

- Score entire skin of the pork shoulder in a crosshatch pattern, with the cuts about 1 to 2 inches apart.
- Rub inside flesh of the pork shoulder with salt and pepper, really working it into the flesh.
- In a small skillet over medium heat, toast fennel seeds until fragrant. Remove from the heat and grind in a spice grinder. Rub ground fennel into the flesh of the pork. Rub in the garlic, red pepper, and lemon zest as well.
- Place rosemary sprigs in the center of the meat, and roll up porchetta. Wrap porchetta in plastic wrap, set in a roasting pan, and let sit in fridge for at least 24 hours, preferably for 3 days.
- Take plastic wrap off porchetta. Unroll porchetta; remove and discard rosemary sprigs.
- Re-roll porchetta and tie off with kitchen twine at about 2-inch intervals.
- Let roast sit for about 1 hour to come to room temperature. Preheat oven to highest temperature: 500° to 550° F.
- Place porchetta, skin side up, on a roasting rack in a roasting pan, and place in oven. Close oven door and immediately reduce temperature to 325° F. The first blast of heat will help brown and crisp the skin. Roast porchetta for about 2½ to 3 hours, rotating the pan every hour, until it reaches an internal temperature of 150° F. Don't turn the porchetta in the rack; keep the skin side up at all times.
- Remove porchetta from oven, tent with foil, and let rest for 15 minutes before carving.

- If the skin somehow didn't get crispy in the roasting process, before you tent it with foil, turn on your oven's broiler, and carefully broil the porchetta on the top and sides until the skin is crisp. Don't let it burn.

- Remove string, slice porchetta, and serve – being sure to include some delicious, crispy skin with each serving!

"ITALIAN" PORK INVOLTINI

Sure, all pork *involtini* are Italian – it's an Italian name for an Italian dish. The reason I've included "Italian" in the name is because of the filling of red, white, and green – like the Italian flag. This dish is not only delicious, but also beautiful.

Serves 4-6

4-5 large Swiss chard leaves – rinsed and dried

1½ pounds pork loin – sliced into 12 thin cutlets

6-8 very thin slices prosciutto

Kosher salt

Freshly ground black pepper

24 strips Peperonata (page 180)

12 very thin slices fresh mozzarella

¼ cup olive oil

12 scallions – white and light green parts, cut into 1-inch pieces

12 asparagus spears – trimmed and cut into 1-inch pieces

¼ teaspoon crushed red pepper

3 Tablespoons dry white wine

2 Tablespoons unsalted butter

- Cut tough center ribs from Swiss chard leaves and discard. Cut each leaf into 2 to 3 pieces, so you have a total of 12 large pieces.
- Using a meat mallet or rolling pin, gently pound pork pieces to $\frac{1}{16}$-inch thick between two pieces of plastic wrap.
- Cut prosciutto into a total of 12 pieces – each about the size of one of the pork cutlets that you have just pounded out.
- Season cutlets with salt and pepper on both sides. On the top of each piece of pork, lay 1 piece prosciutto, 1 piece Swiss chard, 2 strips Peperonata, and 1 slice mozzarella. Roll up pork cutlets individually, and secure each with a toothpick.
- In a large skillet or Dutch oven (must have a lid), heat olive oil over medium-high heat, and brown cutlets on all sides. Work in batches if necessary, removing extra involtini to a plate as you work with the next batch.
- Return all pork and accumulated juices to pan, and reduce heat to low. Add scallions, asparagus, crushed red pepper, and white wine.
- Cover and cook over low heat until pork is completely cooked through, about 8 minutes.

- Transfer involtini to a cutting board, remove toothpick, and slice each in half on the diagonal. Remove scallions and asparagus from pan, and scatter them around a large serving tray. Top with the involtini.
- Reduce the sauce left in the pan over high heat for about 2 minutes. Remove pan from heat, and melt butter into pan juices.
- Pour sauce over the involtini on the serving tray, and serve immediately.

HOMEMADE SAUSAGES WITH SAUTÉED KALE

This is my all-purpose go-to Italian sausage recipe. You can use these sausages in any recipe in this book that calls for Italian sausage. In this recipe – one of the simplest uses for these sausages – they are combined with sautéed greens. Serve this dish with bread, or even *in* bread as a sandwich!

Serves 4-6

1¼ pounds pork shoulder – cubed

4 ounces fresh pork fat – cubed

2 ounces pancetta or bacon – chopped

1 clove garlic – halved

1 teaspoon fresh ginger – peeled and chopped

¼ cup red wine – preferably Chianti

1 Tablespoon Grappa (or Gin)

¼ teaspoon crushed red pepper

1 teaspoon kosher salt

½ small yellow onion – coarsely chopped

1 Tablespoon fennel seeds – lightly toasted

¼ cup olive oil

1 red onion – sliced

4 cups chopped kale and/or collards leaves – tough stalks discarded

¼ cup chicken stock

1 Tablespoon balsamic vinegar

- In a large bowl, combine pork shoulder, pork fat, pancetta, garlic, ginger, red wine, Grappa, crushed red pepper, and salt. Cover bowl; and refrigerate for at least 1 hour, up to overnight.
- Add yellow onions to the pork mixture. Then run pork mixture through a meat grinder back into the bowl so the ground meat mixes with wine and Grappa.
- Add fennel seeds to the ground meat mixture, and mix well with your hands.
- Form the sausages into about 6 to 8 flat oval patties, or stuff mixture into sausage casings. Set aside.
- Heat olive oil over medium-high heat in a large frying pan. Brown sausages on both sides, and then lower heat to medium-low to cook all the way through, about 5 minutes. Remove sausages to a serving plate.
- Pour out all but 2 Tablespoons of fat from the frying pan. Heat fat over medium-high heat.
- Add red onions and sauté until translucent. Add kale, stock, and vinegar, and cook until the kale is nicely wilted and has released most of its liquid.

- Remove kale from the pan and arrange it on the serving plate around the sausage.
- Pour the liquid in the pan over the sausages and kale. Serve immediately with crusty bread.

Roasted Rabbit with Mushrooms, Garlic, Olives, & Rosemary

Too many people in the U.S. have an aversion to cooking rabbit. But in Italy – especially Tuscany – rabbit is an incredibly popular meat. And thankfully so, because it is nothing short of delicious! If you're not ready to step up to eating rabbit, you can substitute a whole chicken, cut up into 8 pieces.

Serves 4-6

2 (2-pound) whole rabbits

1 gallon cold water

Kosher salt

½ cup sugar

1 ounce dried wild mushrooms (porcini or a mixture)

1 cup hot water

Freshly ground black pepper

3 Tablespoons olive oil

1 onion – thinly sliced

1 head garlic – cloves peeled and lightly smashed

20-30 Kalamata olives – pitted and left whole

¼ cup dry white wine

1 cup Chicken Stock (page 173)

4 large sprigs fresh rosemary

- Cut rabbits into 5 pieces each: 4 legs and one saddle/loin piece.
- In a large bowl, mix together cold water, 1 cup salt, and sugar; add rabbit pieces. Cover rabbit with a small plate to keep the pieces submerged. Place bowl in the fridge and allow rabbit to brine for 2 to 4 hours.
- While rabbits are brining, soak dried mushrooms in hot water in a small bowl for 30 minutes to rehydrate. Reserving soaking water, strain mushrooms through a fine mesh sieve to remove grit. Roughly chop mushrooms. Set mushrooms and soaking water aside separately.
- When rabbits are finished brining, drain, and discard brining liquid. Rinse off and completely dry rabbit pieces with paper towels.
- Preheat oven to 375° F.
- Season rabbit with salt and pepper. Heat olive oil in a large skillet over medium-high heat, and brown rabbit pieces, working in batches if necessary. Remove the browned pieces to a 9- x 13-inch baking dish.
- Add onions to the pan, and sauté until translucent. Add garlic, olives, and reserved mushrooms. Sauté until garlic begins to brown.

- Deglaze pan with wine by scraping up all the cooked bits on the bottom of the pan. Cook until the wine is almost completely evaporated.

- Add reserved mushroom soaking water and chicken stock to the pan, and simmer until liquid is reduced by half. Pour liquid, garlic, olives, and mushrooms evenly over the rabbit pieces in the baking dish. Top with rosemary sprigs and cover with aluminum foil.

- Roast in the oven until rabbit is done, about 20 to 30 minutes.

- Remove from oven and allow to rest, still covered, for 10 minutes. Discard rosemary.

- Serve rabbit pieces topped with garlic, olives, and mushrooms, and some sauce from the pan.

Roast Chicken with Lemon & Rosemary

The simplest flavors combine here in a roast chicken you'd swear came right out of the finest Tuscan trattoria. The trick here is to make sure everything is as fresh and of the highest quality as possible – especially the chicken.

Serves 4-6

1 whole chicken (about 3½ pounds)

1 gallon water

Kosher salt

2 Tablespoons unsalted butter – softened

1 teaspoon chopped fresh thyme

1 carrot – peeled

2 celery stalks

1 onion

1 lemon – quartered

¾ ounce whole fresh rosemary sprigs

2 cups Chicken Stock (page 173)

Olive oil

Freshly ground black pepper

2 Tablespoons very high quality extra virgin olive oil

- Trim excess fat off chicken and discard. Remove wing tips and save them for stock. Remove giblets from inside bird and save for another use.
- In a large bowl or pot, mix water and ¾ cup salt together until salt is dissolved. Place chicken in brine, and place in fridge for at least 4 hours.
- While chicken is brining, mix together butter and thyme – set aside.
- Remove chicken from brine, rinse off and dry thoroughly, inside and out, with paper towels. Discard brine.
- Preheat oven to 400° F.
- Coarsely cut carrot, celery, and onion. Place in the bottom of a roasting pan.
- Sliding your fingers under the skin of the breast, massage butter into breast meat, being careful not to tear skin.
- Place lemon quarters and rosemary inside chicken. Truss chicken by tying the wings to the side of the bird, and tying legs together. Place chicken on top of vegetables in the roasting pan. Pour stock into the bottom of the pan.

- Brush bird lightly with olive oil all over - don't miss the thighs! Season with salt and pepper to taste, and roast until thigh meat registers 155° to 160° F on an instant-read thermometer, about 40 minutes.
- Remove chicken from oven and place on carving board. Tent loosely with foil, and let rest for 10 minutes.
- Remove lemon and rosemary from inside bird and discard. Carve bird, drizzle with extra virgin olive oil, and serve.

Roasted Duck Breast with Blood Orange and Apricot Sauce

In France, duck breasts are commonly turned into *Duck a l'Orange*. But in Italy, there is a wide range of dishes made with this awesome meat. For my take on combining duck with orange, I use the flavorful and colorful blood oranges of Sicily and combine them with apricots and Marsala to really make this a dish with Sicilian roots. Be sure to save the rendered duck fat – it can be used in a wide variety of other dishes.

Serves 4

4 (12-ounce) duck breasts

Kosher salt

Freshly ground black pepper

Juice and zest of 2 blood oranges – divided, zest of 1 orange reserved for garnish

8 sprigs fresh thyme

1 small shallot – thinly sliced

½ cup medium-bodied red wine

¼ cup Marsala

½ cup Chicken Stock (page 173)

30 whole dried apricots

2 Tablespoons unsalted butter

- Score skin of duck breasts in a crosshatch pattern, being careful to cut through only the skin – and not too deeply. Pat breasts dry with paper towels.

- Season flesh side of breasts with salt, pepper, and zest of 1 blood orange. Place breasts on a plate and lay 2 thyme sprigs on each breast. Place breasts in fridge, covered, for at least 1 hour, up to 4 hours.

- Preheat oven to 325° F. Remove duck breasts from fridge, discard thyme sprigs and orange zest.

- Heat a large skillet over medium heat. Place duck breasts, skin side down, in the pan. Duck breasts will begin rendering lots of fat. Pour off extra fat from the pan as the breasts cook, reserving fat for a future use. You will likely have to remove fat several times. Continue to cook breasts like this for about 12 minutes to make sure the skin is very crispy.

- When breasts are done on the skin side, flip them over to sear the meat side for about 1 minute. Place breasts, skin side down, in a roasting pan, and finish cooking in the oven. Cook to an internal temperature of 125° F for medium-rare, about 7 to 10 minutes.

- While duck is finishing in the oven, use the skillet the breasts were cooked in to complete the sauce. Pour off all but 1 Tablespoon duck fat from pan. Keep heat at medium.

- Add shallots to the pan and sweat them for 1 minute.

- Deglaze pan with red wine, Marsala, Chicken Stock, and reserved juice from both blood oranges by scraping up all the cooked bits on the bottom of the pan.

- Add apricots, increase heat to high, and reduce sauce while stirring occasionally.

- Remove duck breasts from oven, and cover loosely with aluminum foil. Let rest for 5 minutes.

- Add accumulated juices from the roasting pan to the sauce, and continue to reduce sauce to $\frac{1}{3}$ cup.

- Season sauce to taste with salt and pepper.

- Remove apricots from sauce and place them around the perimeter of a large serving platter.

- Strain remaining sauce into a small bowl, and melt butter into sauce.

- Slice duck breasts thinly. Place skin-side up in the center of the platter with apricots.

- Pour the sauce over the duck breasts and apricots, and garnish lightly with remaining orange zest. Serve immediately.

Cozze di Mare (Steamed Mussels)

This dish is the embodiment of the joy in a simple Italian preparation of a few ingredients that come together in perfect harmony. You could easily serve this dish as an antipasto for six or as a meal for two. Either way, it's a dish that was meant to be shared, and is guaranteed to be enjoyed!

Serves 2-6

2 pounds mussels

½ cup dry white wine

¼ cup Sambuca

½ teaspoon kosher salt

¼ cup heavy cream

½ cup finely diced fennel – some fronds reserved for garnish

2 cloves garlic – minced

2 teaspoons capers – drained and rinsed

1 loaf crusty bread

- Clean mussels, making sure to remove any beards sticking out of the sides. Discard any mussels that won't close up when squeezed a few times. Set mussels aside and keep cool.

- In a large skillet which has a lid, heat wine, Sambuca, and salt over medium heat until it just begins to boil.

- Add cream, fennel, garlic, and capers. Reduce heat to medium-low and simmer for 3 minutes.

- Add mussels, cover pan, increase heat to medium, and allow mussels to steam until they are cooked, about 3 minutes. The mussels will open when they are done. Remove the cover and discard any mussels that did not open. Mix the mussels together with the sauce in the pan.

- Using tongs, remove all mussels to a large serving bowl. Pour all the sauce and vegetables in the pan over the mussels.

- Garnish mussels with reserved fennel fronds. Serve immediately with bread on the side and an extra bowl to hold the discarded shells.

Pan-Seared Italian Sausage with Braised Fennel, Potatoes, and Thyme

My love for fennel knows no bounds. I came up with the concept for this dish when I was in charge of cooking for my staff in my restaurant between shifts, and all I knew was that I really wanted to have some fennel with the meal. So while you may think it was the combination of sausage and potatoes that inspired this dish, it was actually the fennel. No matter how it came about, the result is just marvelous.

Serves 4

²/₃ pound fingerling potatoes – halved lengthwise

1 pound Italian sausage – sweet or hot (or Homemade Sausage – page 142)

2 Tablespoons olive oil

1 onion – julienned

1 bulb fennel – quartered, cored, and sliced

2 cloves garlic – minced

½ cup white wine

¾ cup chicken stock

5 sprigs fresh thyme – left whole, bound with kitchen twine

- Place potatoes in a medium pot. Add lightly salted water to cover and simmer until potatoes are *just* tender. Drain potatoes and set aside.
- In a large skillet (with a lid), sear sausages in olive oil over medium-high heat until browned on all sides. Remove sausages and set aside.
- Reduce heat to medium; add onions and fennel. Cook until onions are translucent.
- Add garlic and cook until fragrant, about 30 seconds.
- Deglaze pan with wine by scraping up all the cooked bits on the bottom of the pan, and then add chicken stock. Bring to a boil.
- Add reserved potatoes, sausages, and thyme sprigs to pan. Cover, reduce heat to low, and cook until sausages are cooked through and fennel is tender, about 20 minutes.
- Discard bundle of thyme sprigs.
- Serve a good mix of potatoes, fennel, and sausage to each of 4 plates. Be sure to drizzle the pan sauce over top of each serving.

Red Snapper nel Cartoccio with Fresh Summer Vegetables

Cooking in parchment (*nel cartoccio*) is not only a healthful way to steam amazing amounts of flavor into your food, but it also makes a fabulous presentation at the table when each guest rips into the parchment paper parcel. Use only the freshest vegetables and herbs here – it makes all the difference!

Serves 6

6 (6-ounce) red snapper fillets

1 Tablespoon extra virgin olive oil

Kosher salt

Freshly ground black pepper

1 zucchini

1 yellow squash

1 red bell pepper

12 Kalamata olives – pitted and sliced

2 cloves garlic – minced

2 teaspoons chopped fresh basil

2 teaspoons chopped fresh oregano

2 teaspoons chopped fresh flat leaf parsley

Zest of 1 lemon

3 teaspoons white wine

<u>Special equipment needed</u>: 6 squares parchment paper – each about 12-15 inches per side

- Preheat oven to 400° F.
- Using tweezers, remove any stray bones in the flesh of snapper fillets. Rub fillets with olive oil, and season with salt and pepper.
- Lay out the 6 squares of parchment paper on a clean dry work surface.
- Using a mandoline set to a thin setting with the julienne cutter in place, shave off the outer layers of zucchini and yellow squash to make "spaghetti" of each. Don't go all the way in to the seeds; discard the seeds. Toss zucchini and squash in a medium bowl.
- Core and seed red pepper, and slice into long, thin strips. Toss with zucchini.
- Distribute zucchini, squash, peppers, olives, garlic, and herbs evenly among the parchment squares.
- Place one fish fillet on each bed of vegetables, and distribute lemon zest equally over the fillets.
- Fold parchment over to make a triangle. Crimp the edges of the parchment, almost all the way, to seal in the fish. When the parchment is mostly sealed, tilt the parchment and pour ½

teaspoon wine into each packet. Finish sealing parchment bundles. (I usually use a stapler to seal the paper, just be sure to remove that before serving.)

- Place bundles on a baking sheet, and cook in the oven until fish is done, about 18 to 20 minutes. (You can check the doneness of the fish by opening one of the packets, and testing the fillet. If one is done, all are likely to be done.)

- Serve the closed packets immediately, allowing guests to open them at the table. Be sure to warn them of the steam that is going to escape!

Salt-Roasted Branzini with Arugula, Prosciutto, and Lemon

Salt-roasting a whole fish produces a real showstopper of a main course as you break into a mound of salt and reveal beautiful cooked fish inside. This can only be done with a whole, skin-on fish – the skin provides the barrier between the meat and the salt that keeps the fish from becoming salty to the point of being inedible.

Serves 2-4

2 (2-pound) whole branzini (or other firm-fleshed white fish) – skin on, cleaned and gutted

4 pounds kosher salt (or inexpensive sea salt)

½ cup water

1 lemon – thinly sliced

4 sprigs fresh thyme

4 bay leaves

1 teaspoon black peppercorns

Garnish:

½ lemon – cut into wedges

2 ounces thinly sliced prosciutto

½ cup arugula leaves

- Preheat oven to 400° F. Line a baking sheet with foil.
- Make sure branzini are gutted and scaled. Using needle-nose pliers, remove bones from the center cavity of the fish. Keep the skin on the fish – this is very important.
- Mix salt and water together in a large bowl to create a mixture that is the consistency of wet sand.
- On the prepared baking sheet, lay down a ½-inch thick layer of the salt mixture large enough to fit both fish on top of it.
- Stuff body cavities of fish with lemon slices, thyme, bay leaves, and peppercorns, evenly distributing between the two fish.
- Lay fish on the salt bed you've created, then cover fish completely with remaining salt. If the tails or heads are sticking out a little, that's okay.
- Roast fish for 25 minutes.
- Remove fish from oven and let rest – still in the salt shell – on the counter for about 10 minutes.
- Crack open the salt shell, and carefully remove fish. Discard lemon mixture inside fish, and brush all salt off outside of fish.
- Lay fish open, remove bones from the fillets of the fish. Remove fillets (with or without the skin) to a serving tray.

- Top each fillet evenly with a spritz of lemon juice, prosciutto, and arugula.
- Serve immediately with lemon wedges.

Dolci

I was only thirteen years old the first time I went to Italy. I think the thing that amazed me most was that meal after meal, oftentimes the only dessert that was offered was fresh fruit. No cakes, pies, cookies, ice cream, or anything that Americans consider to be a traditional dessert – just apples, grapes, and maybe a little cheese. While it was a bit of a culture shock at first to an American kid, I was won over by the concept in no time.

Most Italians don't possess a collective sweet tooth the way we do here. That's not to say they don't like or can't make great desserts. Sicilians make fabulous marzipans that they form into designs to mimic all sorts of other foods. Additionally, I think Northern Italians are the most underrated chocolatiers in the world. The point is that the dessert is not the emphasis of the meal. It's just the sweet, light end to a lovely, leisurely meal with family and friends.

So at last we have come to the end of our meal. Fitting in with the concept of this book, I continue to leave out tomatoes, but obviously that's not an astounding achievement in this chapter. I would like to introduce you to some of my favorite examples of Italian desserts. I hope you enjoy them as a sweet reward for all your great cooking so far!

Strawberries in Balsamic

Balsamic vinegar works well here as the natural flavors in balsamic go together magically with strawberries. A little sugar and a little flavoring, and you have a topping for pies, ice cream, meringues, angel food cake – you name it. For simple elegance, serve the berries on their own with a dollop of whipped cream or zabaglione. If you can find a flavored balsamic – like chocolate or fig – even better!

Feel free to mix and match: Instead of strawberries, try raspberries, blueberries, and blackberries, or stone fruits like peaches, apricots, and cherries. As a topping for vanilla ice cream, there is nothing better.

Makes 2 cups

1 pint strawberries – stemmed and halved

¼ cup balsamic vinegar

3 Tablespoons sugar

Additional flavorings (pick any one of these, or invent one of your own!):

½ vanilla bean – sliced in half lengthwise and seeds scraped

Zest of one orange

1 teaspoon grated ginger

½ teaspoon ground cinnamon

10 fresh mint leaves

- Combine berries, vinegar, sugar, and one flavoring in a bowl. Let marinate, stirring occasionally, for at least 1 hour in the fridge, but no more than 3 though, as berries will begin to break down too much in the vinegar.

- Strain berries, reserving the vinegar they soaked in, and discarding any flavoring items, like cinnamon or vanilla beans, as appropriate.

- Serve over vanilla ice cream with a little of the balsamic sauce, or use with the dessert of your choice.

TIRAMISU

This is my way of making this most classic of Italian desserts. Most people place the alcohol for *tiramisu* in the coffee mixture that is boiled and then soaked into the ladyfingers. While this is nice, I find the alcohol is too subtle in this method, so I mix it into the cream and mascarpone mixture. Strega is very hard to find in the U.S., but if you can find it, its herbal flavors make it the best choice.

Serves 9

2 cups strong coffee

2 large egg yolks

3½ Tablespoons sugar

1½ Tablespoons Strega (or Sambucca)

½ Tablespoon Rum

8 ounces mascarpone cheese

½ cup heavy cream

1 large egg white

Pinch kosher salt

18-25 large Italian ladyfingers – depending on the size of the ladyfingers, you may need anywhere between 30-40

6 ounces whole raspberries – rinsed, dried, and torn in half (or sliced strawberries)

Unsweetened cocoa

- Place coffee in a wide, shallow dish (like a pie pan), and set aside to cool.
- In a medium bowl, beat egg yolks and sugar thoroughly with an electric mixer until very pale yellow in color.
- Add Strega and Rum, and mix in thoroughly.
- Gently mix in mascarpone using the mixer's lowest speed.
- In a small bowl, whip heavy cream; then fold it into the mascarpone mixture.
- Wash off the beaters, and in another small bowl, beat reserved egg white with salt until stiff peaks form. Fold into the mascarpone mixture.
- Soak ladyfingers, one at a time, in the coffee until they are moist, but not soggy, about 5 seconds each. Lay each ladyfinger into the bottom of a 9-inch square glass pan.
- Continue in this way until you have an entire layer of soaked ladyfingers on the bottom of the pan.
- Spoon out a little less than half of the mascarpone mixture and spread it evenly across the top of the ladyfingers in the pan.
- Spread raspberries in an even layer on top of the mascarpone mixture.

- Soak remaining ladyfingers, and create another layer in the pan on top of the raspberries.
- Top with the remaining mascarpone mixture.
- Using a fine-mesh strainer, dust the top of the tiramisu thoroughly with cocoa and set it in the fridge, uncovered, for at least 2 hours, up to overnight.
- To serve, cut into 9 pieces, and place each piece on a small plate. Dust each piece again with cocoa as you serve.

ORANGE-VANILLA PANNA COTTA

This is a double-layer panna cotta which combines the flavors of orange and vanilla in a way that will take you back to the days of chasing down the ice cream truck in the hopes of getting a Creamsicle. Be sure to serve this dessert in glasses so people can see the layers, and then dive your spoon all the way down with each bite to savor the flavors together.

Serves 6

<u>Orange Layer</u>:

1 ¾ cups orange juice – divided

1 ⅛ teaspoons unflavored gelatin powder

6 Tablespoons sugar

¼ cup heavy cream

10 Tablespoons buttermilk

- Pour ¼ cup orange juice into a small bowl. Bloom gelatin by sprinkling it over the surface of the juice. Set aside.
- Meanwhile, in a large saucepan over high heat, heat 1 ¼ cups orange juice and sugar, stirring to dissolve sugar. Boil until syrup is reduced to 6 Tablespoons, about 10 to 15 minutes. Remove from heat.
- Add hot juice to the gelatin mixture in the bowl, and stir until gelatin is dissolved.
- Fill a large bowl with ice cubes. Set a slightly smaller bowl in the bowl of ice. Pour remaining ¼ cup orange juice, heavy cream, and buttermilk into the bowl. Pour in the gelatin mixture and stir to combine. Keep stirring the mixture to cool it down to 50° F.
- Divide the mixture evenly among six water glasses. Be sure to clean any drips from the sides of the glasses. Cover each glass with plastic wrap, being sure not to touch the surface of the panna cotta, and set in fridge until set, about 2 hours.
- Once the orange layer is set, begin vanilla layer.

<u>Vanilla Layer</u>:

1 ⅛ teaspoons unflavored gelatin powder

¼ cup milk

6 Tablespoons sugar

1 cup heavy cream

6 Tablespoons buttermilk

1 ½ teaspoons vanilla extract

- Bloom gelatin powder as before by sprinkling it on top of milk in a medium bowl.

- Fill a large bowl, one larger than the medium bowl you bloomed the gelatin in, with ice cubes.

- In a saucepan, mix sugar, cream, buttermilk, and vanilla. Heat until just simmering.

- Remove from heat, and pour heated cream mixture into bowl with milk and gelatin. Stir until gelatin dissolves. Place bowl into the bowl with the ice, and stir mixture gently to cool the cream mixture to 50° F.

- Layer the vanilla mixture evenly over the set orange layer in the water glasses. Cover each glass with plastic wrap, being sure not to touch the surface of the panna cotta, and set in fridge until set, about 2 hours.

CARAMELIZED POLENTA IN SWEET RED WINE

I told you back in the polenta chapter that the versatility of polenta was hard to beat. Well, here's more proof – a dessert made with polenta and topped with spiced sweetened red wine! The polenta and the sweet red wine can be made ahead of time as well in this recipe, so you only have to do a little work when it is time to serve dessert. You won't need a glass of dessert wine to accompany this one!

Serves 4

2 cups water

6 Tablespoons milk

1 vanilla bean – halved lengthwise, seeds scraped out and reserved

1 cup plus 1 Tablespoon sugar – divided

$\frac{2}{3}$ cup polenta

Kosher salt

1½ Tablespoons butter

1 cup red wine (Chianti or Sangiovese)

½ teaspoon lemon zest

3 whole cloves

1 cinnamon stick

2 Tablespoons roughly chopped hazelnuts – toasted

- Generously grease a small loaf pan. Set aside.

- In a medium saucepan over medium heat, bring water, milk, vanilla bean pod and seeds, and 3 Tablespoons sugar to a simmer. Slowly whisk in polenta and cook at a light simmer, stirring frequently, until the polenta both pulls away from the sides of the pan when it is stirred and is no longer gritty in texture. This will take about 30 to 40 minutes.

- Remove vanilla bean pod and discard. Season polenta to taste with salt, ¼ teaspoon at a time. Melt in butter, and transfer polenta to the prepared loaf pan. Place polenta in the fridge to chill until it has set up completely, about 2 to 3 hours.

- While the polenta is cooling, combine wine, lemon zest, cloves, ½ cup sugar, and cinnamon stick in a small saucepan. Bring mixture to a boil, and reduce to a simmer. Simmer for 7 minutes to thicken mixture slightly. Strain wine sauce and set aside, discarding solids.

Note: You can make recipe to this point ahead of time. Polenta and sweetened wine will keep, refrigerated, overnight.

- When ready to serve polenta, preheat broiler. Line a baking sheet with aluminum foil.

- Remove polenta from the pan. Cut cooled polenta loaf into 1½-inch cubes. In a medium bowl, toss cubes with remaining 6 Tablespoons sugar, and transfer to the prepared baking sheet. Broil polenta (watching closely and turning as needed) until the cubes are well-caramelized, about 12 to 15 minutes.
- While polenta is broiling, gently reheat wine sauce.
- Distribute caramelized polenta cubes among 4 glasses, and then pour warm wine sauce over the cubes. Top with hazelnuts and serve.

Venetian Galani (Sweet Fried Ribbons)

Carnivale in Venice is what we in the United States think of as *Mardi Gras* in New Orleans. It's a vibrant festival of indulgence before the coming of Lent. What better way to indulge than with a load of sweet fried pastries? This is just one of several recipes for the many different fried sweets you'll find in Venice at this time of year.

Makes about 40-50 galani

$\frac{1}{3}$ cup sugar

2 Tablespoons butter – softened

5 large egg yolks

$\frac{1}{4}$ teaspoon kosher salt

6 Tablespoons sour cream

1$\frac{1}{2}$ teaspoons vanilla extract

1$\frac{1}{2}$ Tablespoons Sambuca

2 Tablespoons milk

2 cups all-purpose flour

5 cups vegetable oil – for frying

¾ cup powdered sugar for dusting – or as needed

- In the bowl of an electric mixer, beat together sugar and butter until fluffy.
- Beat in egg yolks, one at a time.
- Beat in salt, sour cream, vanilla, and Sambuca.
- Add milk, and beat on high speed until mixture is uniform.
- Add flour, and beat on low speed for about 3 minutes to develop a little firmness to the dough, but not too much.
- Place dough on a clean, lightly floured surface, and cut into four pieces. Wrap each piece with plastic wrap and let rest in the fridge for 30 minutes to 2 hours.
- Remove one piece of dough from the fridge, and roll out to $\frac{1}{16}$-inch thick.
- Using a pizza cutter, slice dough into 1$\frac{1}{2}$-inch wide strips.
- Cut strips crosswise (preferably with a fluted pastry wheel) into 4-inch pieces.
- In the middle of each piece, cut a 1-inch slit lengthwise. Pull one end of the piece through the slit so that the piece has two twisted sides on either side of the slit, and the whole thing resembles a bowtie.
- In a deep fryer or a large saucepan, over medium-high heat, preheat frying oil to 375° F. Test a small piece of dough first by placing the dough in hot oil. It should become golden on one side

in about 30 to 45 seconds, then turn it over and cook the other side until it's golden as well. Take note of the amount of time it takes to cook the dough pieces.

- Once you know the cooking time for the galani, continue cooking them in small batches until they're all cooked. Drain the cooked galani on wire racks.

- Dust the galani generously with powdered sugar. Serve warm or cool, but definitely serve the same day.

TOASTED PANETTONE WITH LIMONCELLO ZABAGLIONE

Christmas in Italy means it's time for panettone, the marvelous Christmas bread. Panettone, thinly sliced and toasted, topped with butter is nice; but if you top it instead with zabaglione, a sweet, whipped custard, you have something truly divine. This recipe uses my homemade Limoncello, which is also hard to beat!

Serves 6-8

1 pound panettone (about ½ of a small loaf)

3-4 Tablespoons butter – melted

5 large egg yolks

1 large egg

¼ cup + 2 Tablespoons sugar

1½ Tablespoons Limoncello (page 185)

- Slice panettone thinly with a bread knife. You want large, complete slices, if possible, for better presentation.
- Brush slices of panettone with melted butter on both sides, and set aside.
- In a small saucepan, bring ½ cup water to a gentle simmer.
- Prepare zabaglione by combining egg yolks, egg, and sugar in a heatproof bowl. Whisk together thoroughly, about 3 to 4 minutes. Whisk in Limoncello.
- Place the bowl with the egg mixture over the pot of simmering water (make sure the bottom of the bowl doesn't touch water). Gently heat while stirring continually until the mixture thickens, about 2 to 3 minutes. Set aside while toasting the panettone.
- Heat griddle pan over medium heat, and toast slices of panettone until nicely browned on both sides.
- Serve panettone hot with zabaglione drizzled over the top. Of course you can also serve it with some vanilla ice cream if you really want a truly decadent dessert.

SALT CHOCOLATE & ALMOND BISCOTTI

You'll find that the chocolate that works best in this recipe is salt chocolate – a chocolate bar with sea salt flakes in it. The flavors are reminiscent of a chocolate pretzel, only without the pretzel. If you can't find this kind of chocolate, substitute semisweet chocolate chips. If you can find salted chocolate though, buy some extra, because I promise you'll be eating lots of it!

Makes about 40 cookies

20 ounces (4¼ cups) all-purpose flour

2 cups sugar

1 teaspoon baking powder

1 teaspoon baking soda

½ teaspoon ground cinnamon

¼ teaspoon freshly grated nutmeg

1 teaspoon kosher salt

½ cup strong coffee – cooled to room temperature

¼ cup milk

1 Tablespoon water – room temperature

2 large egg yolks

2 teaspoons vanilla extract

1 cup whole almonds – coarsely chopped

12 ounces salted dark chocolate – coarsely chopped (or semisweet chocolate chips)

- Preheat oven to 350° F. Line two baking sheets with parchment paper.
- In the bowl of an electric mixer, using paddle attachment, mix together flour, sugar, baking powder, baking soda, cinnamon, nutmeg and salt.
- In separate bowl, whisk together coffee, milk, water, egg yolks, and vanilla.
- With mixer running on low, pour in wet ingredients. Then add almonds and chocolate. Mix until just combined.
- On a lightly floured work surface, shape dough into four 12-inch logs. Place logs on prepared baking sheets, 3 to 4 inches apart. Bake, rotating pan once, for 25 minutes, or until well set and crispy on the outside. Logs will still be moist in the middle.
- Remove the pan from the oven. Cut the logs crosswise at an angle to make biscotti. Place biscotti back on the baking sheet on their sides with the cut sides facing up.
- Bake for an additional 7 to 10 minutes, until cookies are crispy throughout but not completely dried out and brittle.
- Serve with cappuccino or ice cream, or simply enjoy them on their own.

Extras

These are the useful and delicious little scraps and tidbits that float around in several of the recipes. I figured you'd need them, but I didn't want to write them over and over again, making all of the recipes seem a mile long. The great thing about most of these Extras recipes is that you can make large batches of them, and store them for future use. So it's probably a good idea to make lots of these items in advance, and then use them throughout the book. It's not often that the little touches are the inspiration for cooking more and trying new things, but if that's how it works out for you, then who am I to argue?

CHICKEN STOCK

This stock is the basis for many soups, braises, and sauces; so ensuring that it's good stock is essential to turning out quality foods. The addition of rosemary is what gives this stock a distinctly Italian flair; but even if you leave it out, this recipe will turn out great stock for you every time.

Makes about 1 gallon

2 chicken carcasses – wing tips and neck included, if possible

3 carrots – peeled and roughly chopped

4 celery stalks – roughly chopped

2 large white onions – roughly chopped

8 cloves garlic – halved

½ bunch fresh flat leaf Italian parsley

10 bay leaves

2 Tablespoons black peppercorns

10 sprigs fresh thyme

1 sprig fresh rosemary

- Remove and discard any extra fat on chicken carcasses. Place carcasses in a large pot, and cover with cold water by about 2 inches. Bring to a simmer over high heat, then reduce to a LIGHT simmer – about 1 bubble every second. Using a ladle, skim off and discard any fat and froth that rise to the surface. Continue to simmer, uncovered, for at least 3 hours, and up to 8.

- While the stock is simmering, combine carrots, celery, onions, garlic, parsley, bay leaves, peppercorns, thyme, and rosemary together in a bowl. This is your stock *mirepoix*. Set aside.

- Forty-five minutes before the stock is done simmering, add mirepoix, and gently push it down into the stock (do not stir the stock, or it will become cloudy). Increase the heat to return your stock to a light simmer, and let the stock and vegetables simmer together, uncovered, for at least 30 minutes.

- Line a strainer with cheesecloth. Strain the stock into a large bowl, and discard the solids. If you are not going to use it immediately, cool the stock quickly in an ice bath, by setting the bowl of stock inside a larger bowl filled with ice. (Stock that cools too slowly can breed harmful bacteria, so be sure to cool it quickly if you're not using it immediately.)

Seafood Stock

While it's similar in method to the chicken stock, this stock cooks for a lot less time, uses fresh fennel instead of rosemary, and makes use of the light flavor of leeks. Use the green stalks of the fennel and the dark green leaves of the leek that you would otherwise discard; that way they don't go to waste. Save the white bulb of the fennel and the white and light green parts of the leek for another recipe in this book.

Makes about 1 gallon

3-4 pounds fish bones – heads and tails okay, gills removed (Don't use salmon, mackerel, or other oily fish.)

2 carrots – peeled and roughly chopped

Stalks and greens from 1 bulb fennel – roughly chopped

1 large white onion – roughly chopped

Dark green parts of 1 leek – rinsed thoroughly

6 cloves garlic – halved

¼ bunch fresh flat leaf Italian parsley

10 bay leaves

1 Tablespoon white peppercorns

5 sprigs fresh thyme

- Remove and discard any organs, blood, or gills that may be on the fish bones and rinse bones under cold running water. Place bones in a large pot, and cover with cold water by about 2 inches. Bring to a simmer over high heat, and then reduce to a LIGHT simmer – about 1 bubble every second. Using a ladle, skim off and discard any oil and froth that rise to the surface. Continue to simmer, uncovered, for 15 minutes.

- While the stock is simmering, combine carrots, fennel, onion, leek, garlic, parsley, bay leaves, peppercorns, and thyme in a bowl. This is your stock *mirepoix*. Set aside.

- After the stock has simmered lightly for 15 minutes, add mirepoix, and gently push it down into the stock (do not stir the stock, or it will become cloudy) Increase the heat to return your stock to a light simmer, and let the stock and vegetables simmer together, uncovered, for 30 minutes.

- Line a strainer with cheesecloth. Strain the stock into a large bowl and discard the solids. If you are not going to use it immediately, cool the stock quickly in an ice bath by setting the bowl of stock inside a larger bowl filled with ice. (Stock that cools too slowly can breed harmful bacteria, so be sure to cool it quickly if you're not using it immediately.)

Note: When you make fish stock, you'll want to be sure you are simmering your stock under a fan that vents to the outside of your house. The lingering aromas of this stock can become intense if not vented properly.

TRADITIONAL FOCACCIA

This bread has its roots in Northern Italy, primarily from the region of Liguria, which is also where pesto comes from. The defining characteristic of the bread that turns it into a focaccia is the olive oil that is added to the dough, giving it a rich taste and a flaky texture on its golden, crisp crust. The topping recipe of cheese and herbs is what I use as my go-to simple topping for focaccia, but you can really top this bread with anything you like. Use the dough recipe as a base, and then let your imagination be your guide. So long as you brush the olive oil, water, and salt mixture on top, you can really add anything you want after that.

Makes 1 sheet of Focaccia – Serves 6-8

Dough:

¾ Tablespoon dry yeast

2¼ cups warm water

2 Tablespoons extra virgin olive oil

35 ounces (6⅔ cups) bread flour

2 Tablespoons kosher salt

Rolling/Topping:

¼ cup all-purpose flour

Cooking spray

1 Tablespoon water

2 Tablespoons extra virgin olive oil

1½ teaspoons kosher salt

1½ Tablespoons chopped fresh herbs (chives/thyme/oregano/basil/etc.)

1 Tablespoon grated *Parmigiano Reggiano*

- Combine yeast, water, and oil in the bowl of a large stand mixer. Mix with a whisk by hand to dissolve yeast, and let sit for 2 to 3 minutes to allow yeast to proof.
- Add flour and salt. Mix dough with the mixer's bread hook on low speed for 4 to 6 minutes to make a smooth, cohesive dough ball that has cleaned the sides of the bowl. (If the dough continues to stick to the bottom of the mixing bowl, add a little more bread flour.)
- Transfer dough ball to a clean work surface (with no extra flour!), and knead by hand for about 1 minute to smooth out the dough and make it elastic.
- Transfer dough to a large bowl, coat lightly with olive oil, cover with plastic wrap, and let rise for about 1½ hours until dough is at least double in size.
- When dough is finished rising, spread the ¼ cup all-purpose flour on a clean work surface. Punch down dough, remove from the bowl onto the floured surface, and knead 2 or 3 times

to bring the dough together. Invert the bowl on top of the dough and let dough rest for about 10 minutes.

- Preheat the oven to 375° F. Line a large rimmed baking sheet with parchment paper or a silicone baking sheet. Spray the uncovered interior rims of the baking sheet with cooking spray.

- Roll dough out into the shape and size of the prepared baking sheet. Be sure to roll as many large air bubbles out as you can, as these will make the bread too airy.

- Transfer the dough to the prepared baking sheet by rolling the dough up on the rolling pin, and then unrolling it into the pan. With your fingers, spread the dough out into the corners of the pan as best you can. (It's all right if the dough doesn't quite fill all the corners.) Cover with a lightly damp kitchen towel, and let focaccia rise again for about 30 to 45 minutes.

- For the topping, whisk together water, oil, and salt in a small bowl; set aside.

- Take the towel off the focaccia. With stiff fingers, make a series of indentations all over the surface of the focaccia. Your fingers should push down about three-quarters of the way through the focaccia to make nice, deep dents, but no holes all the way through. Use a brush to spread the oil mixture all over the focaccia – being sure to fill the holes you created.

- Sprinkle on the fresh herbs and Parmesan.

- Bake focaccia for about 20 minutes, rotating once during baking, until well browned all over the top.

- Remove, let cool, and cut as desired. Wrap and freeze any leftovers.

Béchamel Sauce

This sauce is the base for many other great sauces. Melt in cheese, and you have the base for macaroni 'n' cheese. Stir in stock, and you have a wonderful, creamy gravy. Mix it with vegetables, and you have the base for any number of casseroles. It's a sauce you will need to make time and time again, so I wanted to make sure you had it in this cookbook.

Makes about 1½ cups

2 Tablespoons unsalted butter

¼ cup all-purpose flour

1¾ cups milk — warmed

½ teaspoon kosher salt

⅛ teaspoon freshly ground nutmeg

- Melt butter in a small saucepan over medium heat.
- When butter stops foaming, but before it colors, add flour and whisk together to make a roux.
- Reduce heat to medium-low. Cook the roux, whisking to keep it from coloring, until it begins to give off a "buttered popcorn" aroma, about 2 to 3 minutes.
- Add half of the warmed milk to the roux; stir to make a thick, smooth paste.
- Add remaining milk, increase heat to medium, and continue stirring gently until the sauce simmers and thickens.
- Season with salt and nutmeg, and remove from heat.

Roasted Red Peppers

These roasted peppers are a useful base for many dishes, and can add flavor and color to a lot of dishes which usually include tomatoes. This roasting technique also works just fine if you want to roast orange, yellow or even green peppers.

Makes about 2 cups

4 red bell peppers (or as many as you need)

Olive oil

Kosher salt

Freshly ground black pepper

- Preheat the oven to 450° F. Line a rimmed baking sheet with aluminum foil or parchment paper.
- Split each pepper in half lengthwise. Remove all the ribs and seeds.
- Rub the outside of each pepper thoroughly with olive oil, and sprinkle lightly with salt and pepper. Place peppers, cut side down, on the prepared baking sheet.
- Roast peppers until the outsides are very dark — black even. Rotate the pan while cooking to ensure even roasting. This process could take up to 40 minutes. Be patient and let them roast thoroughly.
- Remove peppers from the oven, and immediately place them in a large sealable plastic bag. Seal tightly, and let sit for 20 minutes so skins can steam off.
- Remove peppers from the bag; peel off all skins.
- Cool peppers, and use as needed. If you have extra peppers, they keep well in the fridge for up to a week.

PEPERONATA

This dish is not a side dish, but rather a topping for many other dishes. The best use of peperonata is on bruschetta – the toasted breads so common on the streets of Rome. Mixed with leftover Porchetta (page 138), peperonata makes arguably the best sandwich you've ever had. Pair peperonata with anything you like – it will add a zing to almost any dish.

Makes about 2 cups

4 red bell peppers (or a mix of red, yellow, and orange – no green)

$\frac{1}{3}$ cup extra virgin olive oil

4 cloves garlic – thinly sliced

1 small white onion – thinly sliced

Kosher salt

Freshly ground black pepper

3 Tablespoons red wine vinegar

- Core and seed bell peppers; cut into ¼-inch wide strips.
- Heat olive oil in a large saucepan over medium heat.
- Add peppers, garlic, and onions, and sauté until onions are translucent – don't allow any color to develop.
- Add ½ cup water and season to taste with salt and pepper. Simmer, partially covered, until peppers are softened, about 45 to 60 minutes.
- Reserve 2 Tablespoons cooking liquid. Strain remaining liquid from peppers.
- Transfer to a bowl. Stir in vinegar and reserved cooking liquid.
- Cool and store, using as needed. Peperonata will keep for several weeks in the fridge.

STEAMED ARTICHOKES

This is the easiest way to prep artichokes. The artichoke itself is great eaten straight, dipped in Bagna Cauda (page 22). You can put them on pizzas, in salads, marinate them in vinaigrettes, or use them to make Stuffed Artichokes (page 124). In short, this is the usual first step in artichoke preparation.

Makes 4 artichokes

4 medium artichokes

1 lemon – halved crosswise

- Peel off any scraggily outside leaves from artichokes. Trim bottom stem so artichoke can stand upright. With a large knife, cut off top third of artichoke. Finally, using kitchen scissors, cut thorny tips off remaining leaves.
- Rub all the cut surfaces of artichokes immediately with lemon to keep them from discoloring. Place artichokes upside down in a vegetable steamer.
- In a large pan, bring about 3 cups water to a light boil over medium-high heat. Place the vegetable steamer in the pan, and steam artichokes, covered, for about 30 to 40 minutes.
- Artichokes are done when the base of the artichoke where the stem has been trimmed is tender when a small knife is inserted.
- Remove artichokes from the steamer. Serve immediately if eating as a whole artichoke, or place in an ice bath to stop the cooking if using for another recipe.
- When cool, reach inside artichoke, and pull out the center cone of leaves by pinching and giving them a light twist – they should pop out in a single cone – and discard.
- With a spoon, scrape out the hairy "choke" from the center of the artichoke and discard.
- If the outermost leaves are falling off, remove them to make for a "tighter" overall appearance.

Note: If you want just the artichoke heart for something like a pizza, remove all of the leaves. The base of the artichoke that is left behind is the heart, which you can cut up or leave whole for use in another recipe.

BALSAMIC REDUCTION

This is one of the great garnishing sauces for Italian food. Vinegar is an excellent flavor enhancer in general, but this sweet syrup is not only exceptional at adding flavor, but also has a rich, distinct flavor all its own that is fabulous on savory and sweet dishes alike.

Makes about ½ cup

1¼ cups balsamic vinegar

¼ cup honey

- In a small saucepan over medium heat, combine vinegar and honey.
- Bring mixture to a boil. Reduce to a simmer, and cook down mixture until total volume is ½ cup. Do not simmer too rapidly, or the reduction could burn and ruin the flavor.
- Let the reduction cool completely. Place in a small plastic squeeze bottle for future use.

Oven-Roasted Prosciutto

This recipe is admittedly ridiculously simple, but the resulting crispy, salty flakes of prosciutto are incredible additions to a wide number of recipes used throughout this book. It might be something that you didn't know you could do to prosciutto, so I'm including the recipe here for you to make sure you know how to roast it properly.

Makes about 1 cup

¼ pound prosciutto – thinly sliced

- Preheat oven to 350° F. Line a baking sheet with parchment paper.
- Place prosciutto slices on the prepared baking sheet and roast until crispy, about 10 minutes. The time will vary depending on the thickness of the slices – keep an eye on it.
- Once prosciutto is cool, crumble it, and reserve it for future use.

Herbed Candied Walnuts

These nuts are not just delicious on the Pear and Gorgonzola Pizza (page 49), but they will also dress up any cheese plate, or are good simply as an afternoon snack.

Makes about 1 cup

¼ cup sugar

¼ cup dry red wine

1 cup walnut halves

1 teaspoon finely minced fresh rosemary

2 teaspoons minced fresh thyme

½ teaspoon orange zest

Kosher salt

- Preheat oven to 425° F.
- Line rimmed baking sheet with aluminum foil.
- Combine sugar and wine in a small saucepan over medium heat, and cook until syrupy, about 3 minutes. Stir in walnuts, herbs, and orange zest.
- Pour mixture out on the prepared baking sheet, spreading out nuts evenly.
- Roast until nuts are brown, stirring occasionally, about 6 to 10 minutes.
- Remove from oven, sprinkle lightly with salt, and allow nuts to cool.
- When nuts are cool, break into individual pieces.

LIMONCELLO

Let's end the book in the same way I most enjoy ending an Italian meal – with Limoncello. The process takes about 2 months, but the results are well worth it. You can use Everclear to make this instead of Vodka, but I find Vodka makes a smoother drink, and it's easier to come by. (Just don't use the super cheap stuff!) Yes, this recipe makes a lot, but it stores well in the freezer – and why would you go through so much work to only make 2 or 3 servings?

Makes about 1 gallon

15 lemons

1 (1.75-liter) bottle Vodka

5 cups water

6 cups sugar

- Zest lemons into a large bowl or a 1-gallon plastic container for which you have a lid. Be sure not to get any of the white pith in there!

- Juice lemons and save juice for another use. (You don't need the juice for this recipe, but it would be a shame to see so much lemon juice go to waste…)

- Pour Vodka over lemon zest, and stir to combine.

- Cover the bowl or container and place it in a cool, dark place. Stir (or swirl or shake) the mixture once a day, every day, for 4 to 5 weeks.

- Strain the mixture to remove all of the lemon zest, while, of course, saving the lemony Vodka. Discard zest. Pour Vodka back into the container it has been resting in for the past month.

- In a large saucepan over low heat, combine water and sugar, and heat gently while stirring, until sugar is completely dissolved. Remove from heat and let cool to room temperature.

- Add cooled syrup to Vodka and stir to combine. Place the lid back on container, and return it to its cool, dark place. Stir (or swirl or shake) once a day, every day, again for 4 more weeks.

- At this point, the Limoncello is ready to go! For ease in storage, funnel it into used wine bottles (which you've cleaned and dried, of course – preferably ones with screw tops) or other containers, and place in the freezer. Limoncello should be served ice cold, right out of the freezer.

- As with all the other recipes in this book, I hope you enjoy!

Index